WALKING IN HUNGARY

ABOUT THE AUTHORS

Tom Chrystal was born in Huntly, north-east Scotland, and began walking in the eastern Grampians of his native Aberdeenshire. After leaving school he became a military bandsman, spending a year at the Royal Military School of Music. A career in the civil service followed with precious holidays spent walking in the Pyrenees. He took a year off work to visit mountain ranges in Alaska, Canada and Tasmania and went on to study social anthropology at the London School of Economics. Tom has walked in over 30 mountain and upland areas in 15 countries.

Beáta Dósa was born in Mezőkövesd in north-east Hungary and spent her childhood in the village of Tibolddaróc on the edge of the Bükk National Park. Beáta first experienced the joys of hill walking in the Bükk and Zemplén while a member of the state youth movement or Pioneers. She attended Sárospatak bilingual school and took a Masters degree in History of Theatre at the University of Veszprém. As a freelance translator and interpreter Beáta has worked for Hungarian television and non-government organisations and now works for the British Council. Beáta has walked in the Scottish Highlands and Islands, the English Lake District and Slovakian High Tatra.

Front cover: Approaching Füzér Castle, Zemplén, Walk 16

WALKING IN HUNGARY

by
Tom Chrystal and Beáta Dósa

2 POLICE SQUARE, MILNTHORPE, CUMBRIA LA7 7PY
www.cicerone.co.uk

ISBN 1 85284 352 7

A catalogue record for this book is available from the British Library.

Acknowledgements

This guide would have foundered without the advice and experience of many people. Not all are mentioned here but we would like to thank in particular László Kalmár and András Dorogi of the Magyar Természetbarát Szövetség who helped to untangle the confusing strands of the history of walking in Hungary. Thanks to the following we gained much unpublished local knowledge: Zsolt Bacsó for the Aggtelek National Park; the Bükki family of Hollóháza for the Zemplén; Zoltán Répászky and the Holocén Egyesület for the Bükk National Park; and Sándor Dósa on the workings of agricultural co-operatives. We would also like to thank Mónika Horváth for her helpful comments on Hungarian history; Szabolcs Serfőző for his advice and encouragement; and Erika Komon for bringing our attention to Hungary's challenge walk movement. In addition, the hospitality of Ferenc and Anasztázia Lippert and their son Ferike made the long hard walks around the Bakony worth every kilometre. For their kindness, many thanks to the staff of the Máré-csárda; Éva of Porva-Csesznek turistaház; the Flóriáns of Boldogkőváralja railway halt; and Tibor Bielek. Finally, we thank Joshua Shewan for his patience and the use of his facilities and the Dósa family who provided moral support and countless memorable lunches.

Advice to Readers

Readers are advised that while every effort is taken by the authors to ensure the accuracy of this guidebook, changes can occur which may affect the contents. It is advisable to check locally on transport, accommodation, shops, etc, but even rights of way can be altered. The publisher would welcome notes of any such changes.

CONTENTS

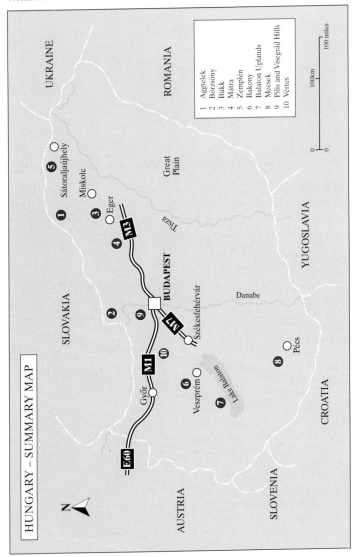

HUNGARY – SUMMARY MAP

1 Aggtelek
2 Börzsöny
3 Bükk
4 Mátra
5 Zemplén
6 Bakony
7 Balaton Uplands
8 Mecsek
9 Pilis and Visegrád Hills
10 Vértes

INTRODUCTION

When you go out into the big forest
Look not behind you
Lest your heart be heavy
As you set foot in a foreign land.

(Hungarian folk song)

THE HIGHLANDS
OF HUNGARY

Every nation projects an image of its landscape to the outside world. In Hungary it is the Great Plain, and most visitors to Hungary are unaware that large areas of the country are covered in highlands and rolling hills with deep wooded valleys, high karst meadows and rocky viewpoints. A walk along the ridges of the Mátra and the Börzsöny or the limestone outcrops of the Bükk will dispel the myth that Hungary is a flat country. Hungary's highland chain of humpback mountains, limestone plateaux and buttes was formed by a combination of volcanic activity and the raising of tropical seabed sediments. There are about 13 000km (8025 miles) of tracks and trails in the hills. For centuries they have been used by medieval miners, Turkish janissaries (soldiers), pillaging Hussites, herders, beekeepers, charcoal-burners and foundry workers. These ancient highways are now a network of walking paths with a system of waymarks first set up in the nineteenth century.

HOW THE GUIDE
IS ORGANISED

This introductory chapter provides practical information about getting to Hungary and what to do on arrival. There is advice on the public transport network, accommodation, maps, the waymarking system and access. Finally, there are introductions to the natural, social and walking history of the hills.

The routes are set out in the guide by region. For simplicity's sake the highland areas of Hungary are divided into two main regions: Northern Hungary (north and east of the Danube) including the Aggtelek karst, Börzsöny, Mátra, Bükk and Zemplén; and Transdanubia (west of the Danube) including the Bakony, Balaton Uplands, Buda Hills, Mecsek, Pilis and Vértes. The summary map of Hungary shows the approximate position of each region.

All the major highland groups of Hungary are described and each region has an introduction including a brief description of the hills and their position, regional history, useful information about how to get there, and points of interest on or near the walks. Individual route instructions provide a short facts section: a summary of the route; walking distance; which map to buy; local public transport; refreshment stops if any; and a brief description of the type of walking to be expected. Distances are initially calculated in kilometres. Miles are given in brackets with the conversion roughly rounded to the nearest half mile. Alternative routes, diversions and quick escapes are clearly demarcated from the main description. Timings are not given as experience suggests that they depend on the fitness of the walker. The walks are not aimed at the incredibly fit, and even the longest route should take no longer than a day at moderate speed. Accompanying the route information is a route map. Every walk stands alone but a few can be linked up to lengthen the route. Hungary's rich and complex history ensures that the walking passes many interesting features from fortress ruins to beehive stones. Points of interest listed in the introduction to each regional section are highlighted in bold in the main text.

Finally, the appendices supply an introduction to the Hungarian language – a list of simple words and phrases to help the English speaker get by in rural Hungary; a glossary to aid Hungarian walking map interpretation; and a list of useful addresses.

GETTING TO HUNGARY

Visas

British visitors to Hungary require a valid passport with at least six months before expiry. Nationals of selected European countries can enter with an identity card – check with the Hungarian embassy for an up-to-date list. Citizens of the European Union do not require a visa for stays of up to six months but citizens of the USA, Canada, South Africa and New Zealand can only stay up to 90 days without an extension. Hungarian border guards are generally not difficult to deal with if you fulfil the above criteria but expect them to be suspicious if you cross the border on foot carrying a backpack. Visa requirements change from time to time – always check the latest position with the Hungarian embassy before making travel arrangements.

Travelling to Hungary

The Hungarian national airline is MALÉV but British Airways, KLM, Alitalia and Delta have regular flights to Hungary although this list is not exhaustive. Flights arrive at Budapest Ferihegy international

Vadálló-kövek, Visegrád Hills, Walk 29

airport. Rail travel across Western Europe can be as expensive as flying, but students and travellers under 26 might consider a European rail pass also valid for travel within Hungary. The over-26 rail pass can be expensive if coming from as far as the UK, Ireland or Scandinavia as the journey to Budapest crosses several zones. Travelling around Hungary by train is so cheap it is probably not worth the outlay. Eurolines runs regular coach services from all over Europe to Budapest, although the journey takes 25 hours from London. If travelling from Western Europe by car the main entry point is through Austria at the busy Hegyeshalom border checkpoint, but expect delays during holiday

periods. Hungary's major highway, the M1, starts from here and it is necessary to pay a toll to use it. (See **Getting Around Hungary** below for an explanation of the system.) If planning a more circuitous route into Hungary – via Slovakia, for example – check with the Hungarian embassy first, as some of these border crossings are for Slovakian and Hungarian citizens only.

Money

The Hungarian currency is the *forint* and can be obtained from a few travel agents in countries of the European Union, but take some cash and travellers' cheques. Exchanging money in Hungary is usually commission-free, but exchange booths at international arrival points always have a poor rate. Ignore approaches from the illegal money-dealers. Hotels and banks also offer poor rates, so shop around the dozens of exchange booths in central Budapest for the best deal. Instant access to cash is easy for holders of ATM or credit cards as cash dispensing machines can be found in cities and larger towns (but not in villages). Internationally recognised cards are acceptable, and machines in Hungary have an English-language option on the display screen. Bear in mind that every time you make a withdrawal your bank back home will probably charge you a transaction fee based on a percentage of the amount withdrawn. Credit cards are accepted in most shops and restaurants in Budapest and other tourist destinations. Credit card fraud is present but probably no higher than any other European country.

Bell tower, Jósvafő, Aggtelek, Walk 1

BUDAPEST

Arriving at Budapest

If arriving by air, Ferihegy international airport is 20km (15 miles) from central Budapest. There are plans to build a train link direct from the terminal to central Budapest, but until then there is an information point in the arrivals building with English-speaking staff. The most expensive options are the door-to-door shuttle service; book at one of the desks in the terminal. A taxi is good value if travelling in a group, but use only the regulated City Taxi and Teletaxi companies who charge a fixed fee. A cheaper option is the airport shuttle bus departing every half hour from the front of the terminal building. It terminates near Deák tér in central Budapest, convenient for the Metro, trams and the 24-hour tourist information office on Vörösmarty tér. This shuttle service stops running at about 11pm. Shuttle bus and taxi drivers speak enough English, but for seasoned travellers looking for the cheapest option catch the municipal airport bus (*Rep-Tér busz*). It also departs from the front of the terminal building, but you will need some loose change or low denomination notes. The driver is unlikely to speak English and the journey terminates at the suburb of Kőbánya, from where it is necessary to get on the Metro (head up the steps of the shopping centre) to continue the journey to Deák tér in central Budapest.

If travelling by train from Western and Northern Europe international arrivals terminate at Budapest Keleti (Budapest East) although a few services arrive at Budapest Déli (Budapest South). Both stations have Metro connections. There are several tourist agencies operating from Budapest Keleti, but head for the Hungarian State Railway (MÁV) information office which is to the right and at the top of the stairs leading down to the main concourse.

International coaches from capital cities in Europe arrive at Budapest Népliget bus station. Take the Metro (Blue Line) for the centre of town. There are left-luggage facilities (*csomagmegőrző*) at Budapest Népliget bus station and Budapest Keleti railway station.

Accommodation

The Hungarian tourist authority, Tourinform, has several branches in Budapest (see Appendix 4) and one of them is open 24 hours. The helpful staff can speak English or German and will gladly provide a copy of their free map of the city and public transport network. Unfortunately Tourinform do not book accommodation, but what they will do is supply leaflets and brochures and point you in the direction of private accommodation agencies who add a booking fee to the price. As long as the familiar big hotel chains are avoided, bed and breakfast at a medium-sized hotel or *panzió* in or near central Budapest can be very reasonable. As the city is a good base for many of the walks in the guide, a family or group might consider a self-catering apartment in the centre of the town. Ask at the accommodation agency for a viewing before you make a decision. For budget accommodation the Tourinform office publishes free booklets listing backpacker hostels and campsites.

Navigating Budapest

The centre of Budapest is a safe and pleasant place to walk around, although the usual warnings about pickpockets and bag thieves apply. Beware of con men posing as plainclothes policemen asking to see your passport. In the event of a problem the 24-hour Tourinform office on Vörösmarty tér will offer assistance and contact the police.

There is an extensive public transport system of buses, trams, trolley buses, Metro and a suburban railway (HÉV). Railway and bus stations with services to walking areas have a Metro connection. Buy a travel pass to get around most of Budapest or, if taking a more relaxed approach to sightseeing, a ten-ticket booklet (*tízes jegytömb*). Otherwise individual tickets for hopping on the occasional tram are very cheap. The universal public transport ticket is available at Metro stations, newspaper kiosks or machine dispensers. A word of warning: a system of self-validation is in operation and it is important to validate the ticket at one of the machines at the top of escalators in the Metro or attached to handrails in buses and trams. There are now posters in English explaining the different types of ticket available and how the system works. Inspectors carry out regular checks and will not accept excuses that you cannot speak Hungarian or were unable to find a place to buy a ticket. If travelling on the HÉV suburban railway, be aware that the little tickets bought in the Metro or in booths are only valid as far as the city boundary which, if heading for Szentendre in order to walk in the Pilis, ends at Békásmegyer. Ticket inspectors on the HÉV seem to be more flexible and will probably only ask for the surplus charge for the rest of the journey, but it is better to buy the full ticket at the station to avoid potential problems.

If you have a few days in the city the Budapest Card will save standing in long queues and dealing with ticket sellers who often speak little English. As well as unlimited public transport travel the card offers free admission to the city's museums and discounts on car hire, the airport minibus, sightseeing tours, excursions and concert tickets. Two- or three-day cards are available from Tourinform offices, Metro stations, travel agencies and hotels. Each card is valid for one adult plus a child under 14.

Shopping and Eating
If self-catering in Budapest, groceries are cheap and there is plenty of variety. Local branches of the corner shop chain *CBA* have most things at a competitive price. There are also large supermarkets in Budapest and the city now boasts the biggest shopping centre in Europe. Late-night corner shops are everywhere and some open 24 hours, although they are more expensive. Head for the southern end of Váci utca for the big indoor market (*Vásárcsarnok*) where bunches of fiery-red paprika, fruit, vegetables, tanks of live carp caught in the River Tisza, and barrels of pickles combine to create a medley of sights and smells.

In the tourist areas there are bars and restaurants and market stalls selling all kinds of gifts, but national specialities such as the famous Tokaj wine or the rather strong spirit made from fruit, *pálinka*, are cheaper in the ordinary supermarkets away from the main tourist drag. If planning to visit the Zemplén do not buy ceramics on Váci utca but visit the factory shop in Hollóháza.

Food and hospitality is central to Hungarian culture but the diversity of traditional Hungarian cuisine owes more to Ottoman and Habsburg domination than to the culinary skills of the nomadic Magyars. Today Hungarians are even more open to outside influences, and eating out in Budapest ranges from fast food to haute cuisine. Vegetarian restaurants and salad bars are a new addition to this traditionally carnivorous culture. Budapest's restaurants and cafés need not be expensive, but if on a budget avoid establishments in the tourist district around Vörösmarty tér and along Váci utca. For a Hungarian experience and a glimpse at the underbelly of Budapest, order a plate of fried fish, sausage and a hunk of bread washed down with a beer from one of the many snack bars up on the gallery of the big indoor market. Before the tradition dies out make sure you try one of the butcher shops (*Hús-hentesáru*); as well as selling meat they offer cheap fry-ups with beer on the premises. Alternatively, explore the side streets for a cheap Hungarian restaurant. In the last ten years there has been a boom in bars catering for expats missing their regular tipple, but for the cheapest drinking and local colour try a typical Hungarian pub, or *söröző*.

Sightseeing

The pock-marks of bullets and shrapnel on a few buildings are a reminder of Budapest's violent past, but extensive renovation work is gradually returning the city to its 1896 grandeur, when it was hailed as Central Europe's Paris. The grandness of the city can best be appreciated on the promenade along the east bank of the Danube. From here the National Palace and castellations of the Fisherman's Bastion provide a dramatic backdrop for this historic

Avas church ruin, Szigliget, Balaton Uplands, Walk 23

15

river. Museums and galleries are cheap, but there are also discounts for children, students, or free entry for holders of the Budapest Card mentioned above. The grand Gothic-style parliament on Kossuth tér is worth a visit, and the Ethnographic Museum opposite has a permanent exhibition about the life and regional costumes of some of the hill peoples described in this guide. On Hősök tere (Heroes' Square) there is a magnificent monument to the Magyar conquest, but if you are interested in some of the less durable heroes of Hungarian history the city's socialist realist monuments can now be viewed at the rather bizarre open-air Statue Park west of Budapest.

If you have a couple of days to spare at the beginning and end of the walking then this is enough time to get a feel for this great city. There are plenty of guides to Budapest – an excellent one is András Török's *Budapest: A Critical Guide* available in the city's many English-language book shops. For free advice have a chat with one of the staff at the Tourinform office who will be glad to give you some ideas about what to see in a limited amount of time and how to get there.

WHEN TO GO WALKING
National Holidays
Europe's Easter, Christmas, New Year and school holidays (mid-June to end of August) will put pressure on accommodation. In addition, Hungarians often head for the hills and book up the walking hostels on the following national days: 15 March (1848–49 Revolution), 1 May (Labour Day), Whitsun Monday, 20 August (Constitution Day), 23 October (1956 Revolution and Republic Day).

Climate
Hungary's climate is a transitional stage between temperate Western Europe and the harsher extremes of the East. Mediterranean air masses raise temperatures in summer and continental air masses lower them in winter. As a result summers can be very hot and winters severely cold, with most precipitation falling in the hills as snow. Walking is possible all year but each season has its pros and cons.

For the walker spring is a pleasant season to get up to the hills, when early flowers brighten the karst meadows, fruit trees are heavy with blossom and the forest full of birdsong. Hungarians often complain that spring is too short, and the transition from winter to summer does seem quite rapid. It can be cool in the evenings and wet at times but expect warm weather as March progresses. Summers are long – the hot weather begins in April and lasts into early October. Midsummer temperatures can rise to 35°C (95°F) but cold fronts pass through from time to time bringing respite from the heat. Summer brings occasional thunderstorms, but hot and dry weather is the norm. The best time to go in summer is May or June when the greenery is still fresh, or August when the meadow flowers are in full bloom. Walkers who prefer cooler weather should consider autumn, when the northern hills experience a refreshing chill from about mid-September.

Expect more rain, but from mid-October the autumn colours in the forests are spectacular. In November the clocks change and there is less daylight walking time. Winter temperature in the hills is on average 5°C (41°F) but on extreme days it can drop to -20°C (-4°F), although the high slopes escape the temperature sink effect experienced on the Great Plain. The northern hills are the coldest and expect snow between late November and March. In Hungary, as in the rest of Europe, the winter snow line has receded and there are now longer periods without cover than there were in the past. Winter weather is stable: if a day starts crisp and windless in the morning it is likely to remain that way all day. Walking across deserted trails through frozen snow is very rewarding, but many of the routes in the guide are written with longer daylight hours in mind. Hungary's highlands do not experience alpine-style hazards, but only experienced hill walkers should venture into the

Badacsony, Balaton Uplands, Walk 23

hills in winter. It is also the hunting season, so keep clear of the hills at dusk and dawn and stay on the waymarked routes.

CLOTHING AND ACCESSORIES

No special clothing or equipment is required to walk in Hungary. Veterans with hard feet will find that a sturdy pair of training shoes will suffice in summer and autumn, although light leather walking boots or at the very least fabric boots are recommended. During prolonged wet spells wear boots, as the trails can get very muddy, and in winter snow lies deep and gaiters are useful. In summer wear light cotton clothing and a sun hat with an ample brim to protect the neck, and if fair-skinned apply sun block. Whatever the season take a waterproof jacket. Shorts are ideal in summer but be aware of ticks (see **Health**). In winter wear layers and a warm hat. Take a torch for emergency night navigation. On long walks in summer carry about two litres of water per person if there are no resupply points along the way. In villages summer dress is casual; shorts and T-shirt are perfectly acceptable but be sensitive if visiting a place of worship.

RURAL ACCOMMODATION

There is something to be said for walking into a village and looking for a room, but without a command of basic Hungarian it is not always easy to find one. With the exception of the shores of Lake Balaton, where a *zimmer frei* (vacancies) notice screams at you from every gate, Hungarian villagers are slow to advertise their spare rooms. If you feel confident enough speaking some Hungarian the village pub is a good place to ask, where the locals will try to help.

As a precaution start at one of Budapest's branches of Tourinform (see Appendix 4) whose English-speaking staff will provide accommodation brochures and advice on where to stay. The branch at Király utca specialises in rural accommodation. Regional offices maintain their own databases of local accommodation and might be able to provide a brochure or offprint. The types of accommodation available in the hills are described below, starting with the cheapest.

Wild Camping

Although this is a good way of getting deep into the hills and probably the only way of seeing the more secretive of Hungary's mammals and birds, wild camping is not permitted in many walking areas. Nature Guards regularly patrol national park land and they have the power to fine and evict offenders. Outside national parks it is also illegal for foreigners to camp in forested areas without permission, and for safety reasons it is inadvis-

Forest cottages, Óbányai-völgy, Mecsek, Walk 25

able to wild camp during the hunting season (October–January).

Official Campsites and Chalets

There are two symbols on Hungarian walking maps denoting a campsite but their exact meaning is not always clear. As a rough guide the wigwam symbol (*sátorozóhely*) on Hungarian walking maps is a designated site that has few or no facilities and, depending on the circumstances, means that you can pitch a tent and perhaps light a fire free of charge. Unfortunately there are few such sites and the ones that are free have become overgrown. The other symbol, a triangle in a semi-circle (*kemping*), is a pay-site with full facilities and often has little wooden chalets for hire. Tourinform publish a free brochure listing pay-sites, although it is not comprehensive as many householders offer camping spaces in their back garden. The phrase to ask whether there is a place to put your tent is *Van sátorhely?* The most campsite intensive (and expensive) region is along the shores of Lake Balaton. Pay-sites usually have good facilities including showers, kitchens and laundry points, but for a little extra you could find a decent room. The campsite season in Hungary is short and geared to school holidays.

Kulcsosházak

Literally 'key houses', these self-catering cottages scattered around Hungary's hills are situated in peaceful surroundings. Depending on your attitude to comfort it is a cheap way for a group of people to live close to the walking routes. The houses are often run by walking clubs or trade unions, but many are available to non-members and are popular with families and students. Facilities are often primitive; there is no running water or indoor toilet, although there are cooking hobs running on gas cylinders. When unoccupied the cottage is locked and the address and telephone number of the keyholder is on a noticeboard near the door,

19

which is not very useful as by this time you are already a long way from the town where the warden lives. Unfortunately most of the keyholders do not speak English; booking has to be done weeks in advance in writing, and the houses are usually booked up months ahead for the summer and Christmas holidays. It is, however, an option worth considering if you know any Hungarians who can do the booking for you.

Walkers' Hostels

Budget accommodation for walkers is limited in Hungary but it is still possible to stay in a *turistaház* or *turistaszálló*. They are marked on walking maps as a black rectangle with a little flag, and the word *turistaház* is usually translated as youth hostel. These establishments, many of which are former hunting lodges, are not members of the International Youth Hostel Association but are run by walking clubs, trade unions or state-controlled industries. Check at the local tourist office if you are expecting to stay at one of these establishments as some hostels marked on Hungarian walking maps are now out of use or are limited to pre-booked group hire. On the other hand, not all hostels are marked on the maps. The best ones are up in the hills away from the main roads, but most can be approached by car.

Hostel facilities are basic but clean and have hot showers, toilets and a canteen, although some establishments are beginning to look run down. Breakfast, lunch and dinner are available at extra cost, after which the price can compare with a private room in a village. Guests can eat their own food in the canteen or have communal cooking facilities. There is no curfew and drinking in the bar will go on into the night until someone complains or the warden (who also runs the bar) wants to get to bed. If you want to make a very early start the next day let the warden know as he probably locks the doors at night. Wardens do not speak English but many hostels have a friendly atmosphere, although do not expect to be surrounded by serious walkers and climbers nowadays.

Üdülő

An *üdülő* is another type of hostel. At best it is an old lodge set in pleasant surroundings, but many are rather utilitarian structures thrown up quickly during the 1950s. The *üdülő* dates back to the Communist period, when each state company ran its own recreation centres for the exclusive use of its workers. A few of these establishments are now open to outsiders. Accommodation is dormitory style, although there are more expensive family rooms. While these establishments are showing signs of decline, the bedding provided is clean.

Meals are of variable standard and add considerably to the cost. For some reason an *üdülő* is often more expensive than a *turistaház*. In summer large parties of children take over this type of hostel. If that is the case it is wise to avoid them, because even if you manage to get into a private room the largely unsupervised children will keep you up all night. It is all a matter of luck and season. A room in the village will probably be cheaper and more pleasant.

Establishments calling themselves a *turistaház*, *turistaszálló* or *üdülő* as well as hostels run by the state railway company and a few affiliated campsites are listed in the rarely updated *Természetbarát Szálláshelyek* published by Hungary's main walking club, the MTSZ, or the Union of the Hungarian Friends of Nature. The book is available from the Cartographia map shop (see Appendix 4). For other budget accommodation the free Tourinform booklet *Ifjúsági Szálláskatalógus* is rather limited, as it only lists hostels affiliated to the International Youth Hostel Association, few of which are near walking routes.

Private Rooms and Apartments

When passing through a village, look for the following signs: *szoba kiadó*, *zimmer frei* and *apartmen frei*. Many private households offer a clean room or apartment with clean bedding for a reasonable price, although meals are not usually available.

Alternatively rent a room or apartment in a family house registered with the Falusi és Agroturizmus Országos Szövetsége (Hungarian Federation of Rural Tourism). Look for their logo (intertwined red and green hearts) on garden gates. Their free catalogue in Hungarian, English and German is available at their Budapest headquarters in Király utca (see Appendix 4). Booking accommodation is not strictly part of their service but they will, if pressed, telephone a householder for tourists who cannot speak Hungarian. Many of the properties in the scheme are also listed on the Centre of Rural Tourism website (see Appendix 4) which has an English-language option. Their packages also include hands-on farming experience, green tourism and activities geared to children. Depending on the set-up you will either share bathroom facilities with the family or hire a separate apartment with *en suite* bathroom and kitchen. Price per night is reasonable, but expect it to rise during public holidays, especially Christmas and Easter. Meals are often available for an additional charge. You are not obliged to eat your host's food but do let them know in advance if you require feeding. If you cannot speak Hungarian there will be some silences at dinner, although it

Villagers, Regéc, Zemplén, Walk 18

is rarely awkward as the house-holders in the scheme are usually friendly. Some families will ply you with wine all night and insist on speaking to you in pidgin German.

Vendégház; Panzió; Szálló/Hotel/Fogadó

These are lumped together because prices and facilities often overlap. The standard of guesthouses and hotels in rural areas is usually excellent and, although more expensive than budget accommo-dation, are good value for money. Prices quoted are for the room, and solo travellers will have to pay the full price for occupying a double room. A *vendégház*, or guesthouse, can be as expensive as a hotel or as

cheap as a *turistaház*. It is a rare practice and not officially con-doned, but beware of establish-ments with dual-pricing systems penalising foreigners. Guesthouses often have access to a kitchen and dining room for self-catering, although home-cooked meals are also available at extra cost.

A *panzió* is a small- to medium-sized hotel offering bed and breakfast and may also have a restaurant and bar for non-resi-dents. A hotel or *szálloda* is the most expensive option. A selection of *panziós* and hotels are marked on Hungarian walking maps. A *fogadó* is Hungarian for inn and is not an indication of price. The local tourist office will provide a list or brochure of accommodation for their area, although a small number of guesthouses and hotels is listed in the MTSZ publication *Természetbarát Szálláshelyek* mentioned above.

GETTING AROUND HUNGARY

Driving

Hungary is not a large country and many walking routes are about an hour's drive from Budapest. Driving is a comfortable way to get to the walk-in points and there are circular walks in the guide ideal for car users. With few exceptions there is always somewhere to park free in a village. Car hire is available at the airport but one of the many travel companies in Budapest can arrange it for you. Road surfaces on motorways and major roads are generally of a high standard but deteriorate as you enter Budapest. Many village streets and back roads are unsurfaced.

The downside of driving on Hungary's smart new motorways is the toll (*autópályadíj*) which is payable on the M1 and the M3. Purchase a sticker (*matrica*) at a toll office at the entrance to the motorway or the nearest petrol station. Look for the sign: *Autópálya matrica kapható*. Ask *Van egy árlista angolul?* for the English-language leaflet explaining the system and latest charges. Stickers are also sold at many post offices or offices of the

Magyar Autóklub (Hungarian Automobile Association). When buying a sticker you will be asked to fill in a registration form. Display the sticker prominently on the windscreen as it will be scanned by special cameras along the highway. There is a heavy fine for not paying. If travelling frequently it is worth buying a nine-day (*heti*) or monthly (*havi*) ticket.

Points worth mentioning about driving around Hungary: third-party insurance is compulsory; driver and passenger(s) including passengers in the back seats must wear seat belts; children under the age of 12 may not travel in the front and must use a child seat; and outside built-up areas dimmed headlights are compulsory during daylight hours. The speed limit is 50km/h (30mph) in built-up areas; 90km/h (55mph) on other roads; and 130km/h (80mph) on the motorway/ highway. The police regularly set speed traps and also carry out spot-checks so always have all your documents, including passport and motorway toll registration form, with you while driving. A hazard to look out for on some main roads and rural areas is poorly visible horse-drawn carts.

Parking space is becoming increasingly limited in Budapest and traffic wardens patrol the streets to catch people whose parking meter ticket has expired. In the worst cases the local authority tows away offending cars. If you are involved in a car accident while in Hungary report it to the police, as damaged vehicles attempting to leave the country without a certificate will be detained. Drinking even the smallest amount of alcohol while driving is an offence.

Public Transport

All the walking research in this guide has tested the feasibility of using public transport to get on and off the walking routes. During the 1950s many waymarked routes were set up to start and finish at a train station or bus stop, reflecting the emphasis on cheap holidays as well as the lower levels of car ownership. Nowadays it is still possible to come out of the forest to a lonely stretch of road and find a bus stop with frequent services, but do not depend on it. Using public transport is also a good way of getting to know a country and it is a safe way to travel in Hungary. The guide attempts to ensure that a route does not leave a walker stranded and that there is ample opportunity to catch a bus or train back to a town or, failing that, there is likely to be accommodation nearby. Whether travelling by bus or train, avoid Friday afternoons. The introduction to each region in the guide provides details about local public transport, but the following is a general introduction to bus and train travel in Hungary.

Rail

The Hungarian State Railway (MÁV) has a large network radiating out from Budapest to many walk-in points. Get to the ticket halls of Budapest's mainline stations well in advance of departure to avoid long queues. A more relaxed method is to buy tickets in advance at MÁV's air-conditioned central booking office (see Appendix 4). Ask for an English-speaking member of staff. Ticket-sellers and inspectors are unlikely to speak fluent English but are usually patient when dealing with phrasebook Hungarian. There are no complicated saver tickets and cheap returns; price is calculated by the kilometre. For student concessions travellers must hold a European rail pass bought in their country of origin.

Ordinary trains are quite efficient but expect to stand in the corridor on many journeys. First class is an alternative, but sometimes the standard is very poor and not worth the extra cost. Services are classed according to their speed and how often they stop: *gyors* (fast – stops at main stations only); *sebes* (stops at smaller towns); and *személy* (stops at every halt). Air-conditioned Inter City trains ('IC' on timetables) are fast and comfortable but you must reserve the seat and pay a booking fee. Specify if you do not want to sit in the smoking coach: *nem dohányzó*. To find

Cave house museum, Szomolya, Bükk, Walk 11

your seat on an Inter City train examine the ticket for the coach (*kocsi*) and seat (*hely*) numbers. With a few exceptions, such as lines with unmanned stations, you will be fined for boarding a train without a ticket. Small red trains (*kispiros*) operating from provincial railway stations get closer to some walking routes. Some hills can be accessed using the little forest trains running from Easter to mid-October.

Summary of railway stations in Budapest and the walking areas they serve:

Budapest Keleti Pályaudvar (Eastern Railway Station): Aggtelek, Bükk, Mátra, Zemplén

Budapest Nyugati Pályaudvar (Western Railway Station): Börzsöny, Pilis

Budapest Déli Pályaudvar (Southern Railway Station): Bakony, Balaton, Mecsek, Vértes.

Bus

Most long-distance buses are comfortable, efficient and air-conditioned, and a pleasant way to get to the hills, but many villages can only be reached by changing for a local bus at smaller towns and provincial capitals. Villages that are popular tourist destinations can be reached by direct bus, but there are likely to be only a couple of services a day.

Rural timetables are often geared to commuting workers, therefore morning buses depart at an unearthly hour. To avoid becoming stranded plan your journey carefully. Pre-booking for long-distance services is possible at city bus stations and will allow you to get on the bus before everybody else and secure a seat; but make sure you are there well before departure. For rural buses, have plenty of small change ready. Country bus drivers do not speak English, but the digital display will show the price of the ticket; or, on the older buses, have a look at the ticket itself. It is rare but inspectors can flag down the bus in the middle of nowhere so do not overstay your journey.

Summary of bus stations in Budapest and the walking areas they serve:

Budapest Népstadion: Aggtelek, Bükk, Mátra, Zemplén

Budapest Árpád híd: Börzsöny, Pilis

Budapest Népliget: Bakony, Balaton, Mecsek, Vértes.

Timetables

National railway and bus timetables (*menetrend*) are available at rail and bus stations, and regional versions can be bought at provincial offices. Tourinform offices have a set of timetables and staff will be glad to help with travel plans. For both train and bus services the summer timetable begins in early June and the winter timetable takes over from September. All times are in the 24-hour clock. If planning your trip from outside Hungary check the railway and bus company websites (see Appendix 4). The

MÁV website has up-to-date timetables and prices in English, but the VOLÁN equivalent is in Hungarian, although it does provide an on-line Hungarian–English dictionary.

Every main railway station has a map of the national network and a timetable for every line, but a few rural railway halts do not have a booking office or timetable, so take a note of the return services before setting off. The national bus network is decentralised and its timetables show only the regional destinations and arrivals.

Hungary's timetables are afflicted by a plague of footnotes. Understanding this cluster of symbols and letters could be crucial if you are not to discover that the last bus you thought you could catch does not run on weekdays. Appendix 2 has a few examples. As a general guide no symbols next to a departure time means the service is daily and a crossed hammer symbol or the letter *M* means that the service runs only on working days.

HEALTH

General

At the time of writing emergency and out-patient treatment are available free to citizens of the European Union, but follow-up care must be paid for or pursued back home. It is worth checking the latest position with the Hungarian embassy before departure. There is no reciprocal health agreement for citizens of the USA, Canada, Australia, South Africa and New Zealand. Whatever your status travel insurance is recommended. Doctors usually speak English, although receptionists and nurses do not. Take a simple first aid kit comprising plasters, bandage, safety pin and anti-histamine for insect bites although all these items are available in Hungarian drug stores. In Hungary only pharmacies (*gyógyszertár* or *patika*) are authorised to supply medicines taken internally, and antibiotics require a doctor's prescription. Pharmacies will accept foreign prescriptions if you require resupply during the holiday. Medicines for personal use up to a certain value can be brought into Hungary. Check with the embassy for the latest regulations.

Ticks

Walking in Hungary is relatively safe, but as with most of Central Europe its forests and meadows are a haven for ticks (*kullancs*), which attach themselves to the undergrowth waiting for a host to pass by. The bite is painless, but an attached tick must be removed promptly and with care so as not to increase the risk of infection. Ticks are active in Hungary from April until the first frost, which can be as late as November, but the main season is May and June. The risk of contracting disease is low for the walker

who follows well-beaten trails, uses a DEET insect repellent, and does not wild camp, but if spending a long time in the hills it may be worthwhile getting vaccinated against encephalitis. Lyme disease can be treated with antibiotics if caught at an early stage, although vaccination is available in the USA.

Dogs

In rural Hungary dogs are not pets but inexpensive alarms, and most houses have a sign on the gate: *Harapós a kutya!* or *Vigyázz! A kutya harap!* (Beware of the Dog). Every garden dog feels it is its duty to bark, howl and snarl at any stranger, and once the first dog starts a chain reaction sets in until the whole village is in commotion. Villagers seem to be impervious to the racket but it is unsettling for the first-time walker in Central Europe. Fortunately the brutes are usually safely locked behind garden gates and it is rare to see feral dogs wandering around the countryside. If confronted by an overzealous village defender that has slipped its chain a threatening swipe with a stick or well-aimed stone should be enough to send it on its way.

The risk of rabies (*veszettség*) in Hungary is very low and health authorities take the control of the disease very seriously. Rabies posters of a fox's head pinned to trees in some walking areas look alarming, but they are merely informing walkers that bait with a serum has been laid in the area as part of a humane programme to vaccinate foxes against the disease. It is unusual to catch rabies in Hungary as owners are legally obliged to vaccinate their dogs regularly. If you are bitten try to identify the dog's owner and insist on the vaccination certificate (*Oltási papírok*) and take it with you to the hospital or nearest surgery. The doctor will administer a tetanus injection whatever the dog's vaccination history, but if you cannot produce a certificate, or the dog was feral, you will be automatically treated for rabies. There is also a follow-up investigation by the local health authority. Treatment for dog bites is considered an emergency and free if your country has a reciprocal health care agreement, but avoid the risk of a bite and the subsequent bureaucracy: steer clear of dogs however friendly they look.

Snakes

The common viper *Vipera berus* can be found in many hill areas, especially in the Zemplén, but it is unusual to see one, let alone get close enough to be bitten, and fatal bites are rare. The anti-venom serum is available at rural pharmacies. If the pharmacy is closed ring the bell for the pharmacist, who usually lives on the premises.

Drinking Water

Karst formation has diverted surface water underground in many upland areas and there are few clear streams. It is not advisable to drink stream water, and not all waterborne diseases can be eliminated using the ordinary purification tablets available in camping shops. In summer carry at least two litres of water per person and fill up whenever possible from the blue pumps found on village streets. Alternatively, the local bar will gladly refill your water bottle from their tap, or if you see a villager working in the garden ask: *Kérhetek egy kis vizet?* (May I have a little water?)

If the route does not pass through villages there are many springs (*forrás* or *kút*) marked on walking maps. They range from boggy hollows to elaborate structures built by the local walking club and named after some local worthy or historical figure. Springs and wells above and away from settlements and hunting lodges are likely to be clean, although there are concerns about the quality of water in parts of the Mecsek. Springs or pumps designated undrinkable are marked: *nem ivóvíz*.

Refreshment Abuse

Some walks pass through villages where cheap bars and excellent restaurants offer food and drink at very reasonable prices. Stopping for refreshments is a pleasant way to break up a walk and Appendix 2 lists a few drinks and how to order them in Hungarian. If you decide to take the opportunity for an extended lunch be aware that excess alcohol is dangerous on a long hot walk. You might also find yourself regretting it as you stumble through the dark to finish the route.

WAYMARKING

Hungary's hundreds of trails are marked out by a system of rectangular coloured waymarks comprising two white bands with a central stripe of red, blue, green or yellow. Auxiliary routes use other symbols: a cross connects two routes; a square leads to a settlement or accommodation such as a hostel; a triangle indicates the route to a summit or viewpoint; an L is the way to a historic ruin such as a fortress; a coloured spot leads to a spring or well; a semicircle to a circular route; and an omega symbol leads to a cave. In ski resorts coloured saltires (stiles with a cross-piece) mark the ski routes. Waymarks are usually painted on trees, but on tree-less heath and karst rocks do the job, and in villages telegraph poles, fence posts, garden walls or water pumps are employed. A few routes have wooden signs giving directions as well as estimated walking times in hours (*ó*) and minutes (*p*).

Hungary's first waymarked routes were set up in the second half of the nineteenth century by volunteers, but it was during the Communist period that state-sponsored organisations took an interest

Volunteers clearing the trail, Börzsöny, Walk 4

in their maintenance. During the 1950s volunteers from the trade unions were deployed around the countryside to repaint the old way-marks and create new routes. In those days the work was paid; transport, brushes and paint were provided free. Nowadays the upkeep of waymarks and monitoring of the routes depends on the availability of walking club members prepared to spend their spare time and money. As a result the coverage varies and many rarely used trails are overgrown and waymarks missing. Sections of the way-marked system follow main roads for a few kilometres. This was not a problem in the 1950s, but the increase in car ownership in recent years has made some road-verge walking unpleasant; Hungarian drivers seem reluctant to give a comfortable distance between themselves and pedestrians. To get the best of an area this guide directs the walker along the most suitable waymarked route and not necessarily the traditional routes prescribed by Hungarian walking guides written in the 1950s.

MAPS

The theory is that if you keep to one waymark colour you need only continue to the end of the route. In practice waymarks tend to be conspicuous when the track is obvious and absent at complicated junctions. Waymarking is improving, but

many were painted a long time ago and are obscured by vegetation, weathered, or the trees they were on have been felled. Old green way-marks tend to turn blue with age and vice versa. Therefore the ability to read a map is important and also adds to the enjoyment of walking. The Hungarian company Cartographia publishes a series of excellent walking maps (*turistatérkép*) in 1:40 000 and other scales. Official walking routes are denoted on the maps as red lines and the different route colours are distinguished by a letter: K (*kék*=blue), P (*piros*=red), S (*sárga*=yellow) and Z (*zöld*= green). A selection of hotels, hostels, campsites, country restaurants, snack bars and even petrol stations are also marked on the maps. Understanding map references is useful for one or two walks in the guide, and an ability to use a compass is helpful at complicated forest trail junctions where visibility is restricted but not essential.

In Hungary Cartographia's maps can be bought in most book shops in cities and towns, but the main stockist is their shop in Budapest (see Appendix 4). Apart from the most tourist-aware settlements small village shops do not usually stock walking maps, but try the post office, any large hotels in the area or the local museum. The relevant map name and number for a specific region is at the beginning of each route description.

Cartographia's maps are fairly accurate and updated regularly, but be aware that even the most recent issue cannot keep up with all changes caused by privatisation. The following points are worth noting.

- With the exception of the Balaton map only a selection of the more common symbols are explained in Hungarian map keys. Refer to the glossary in Appendix 3 for a translation of the symbols and common topographical terms.

- The letter H within a square is a hotel and not a hospital. A hospital or doctor's surgery is a cross within a circle.

- Hungarian maps are fragile and will soon fall apart. Map cases are fine but expensive, add bulk and weight, and are not indestructible. A strong clear plastic bag is adequate protection from rain or perspiring fingers and is inexpensive to replace.

- A common error is to assume that the red lines on the map (the official waymarked routes) will be very obvious on the ground. Unlike the faint dotted lines on the map denoting tracks, the red lines tend to stand out, but they might be less obvious on the ground.

- In a few examples the superimposition of the red lines on the map can be inaccurate enough to place the waymarked route on the wrong side of a stream or valley. It is not a common problem but the knack to not getting lost in the forest is to balance waymark awareness with good map reading.

- Military maps (*katonai térkép*) in the standard 1:50 000 and 1:25 000 scales are available in a few specialist shops in Budapest. There is really no need to buy these more expensive maps as the walks in this guide are covered by the Cartographia series, which is sufficiently accurate for following waymarked trails.

FORESTRY, HUNTING, NATIONAL PARKS, PRIVATISATION AND ACCESS

Forestry

About 15 per cent of Hungary is covered in woodland, most of which is in the hill country. The state planted a third of today's forest in the 1940s, although many clear-cut areas have since regenerated naturally. The state continues to manage over half of the forests, but the little forest trains no longer haul tonnes of timber down from the hills. Since the 1980s there has been more selective felling and an increasing emphasis on conservation. Forty per cent of forest is now in private hands or belongs to those agricultural co-operatives that survived the changes after 1989. Forestry operations during the week are a fact of life and a route may be closed for safety reasons. There is usually an alternative route to get around the obstacle.

Hunting

As you wander along the trails you will see many hunting hides that resemble sinister prison camp watchtowers. Detailed maps of game reserves drawn up centuries ago are evidence of Hungary's long relationship with hunting, and in the fifteenth century King Matthias stocked his reserves with lions. Game management declined during the turbulent Habsburg–Ottoman wars. As late as the 1940s, Miklós Horthy, the Regent of Hungary, went as far as evicting tenants in order to turn his estate into a bear reserve. Despite the egalitarian ideology of the Communist era, hunting continued to have overtones of privilege and high-ranking party members met in the Zemplén for hunting weekends. Nowadays, foreigners pay good money to shoot game in Hungary. The season for most game is between 1 October and 31 January, but walkers who keep to waymarked trails and stay out of the woods between dusk and dawn are unlikely to encounter hunters. Look for the following type of notice: *Figyelem! Belépni 16-09 között életveszélyes és tilos!* This warns people to stay away from an area between 4pm and 9am.

View from Három-kő, Bükk, Walk 9

National Parks and Protected Areas

Hungary boasts many national parks and they provide a refuge for the nation's rarest flora and fauna. The territory of a national park or other specially protected area is delimited on walking maps using red dots. On the ground a sign with an egret symbol marks the entrance to a national park, although some regions have their own symbol: the fire salamander in the Aggtelek; and the carline thistle in the Bükk. Look for the letters NP (*Nemzeti Park* – National Park); TVK (*Tájvédelmi Körzet* – Landscape Protection Area); and TVT (*Természetvédelmi*

Terület – Nature Conservation Area). Many walks in this guide pass through national park land and other conservation zones, so keep to the waymarked paths and access will not be a problem. Red hatching on a walking map or the words *Nem látogatható!* (No visitors!) denote highly restricted areas where rare birds are nesting. Do not be tempted to enter these zones hoping to see rare species as the restriction might be for another reason such as hidden mine shafts dating back to the eighteenth century. Note that all caves in Hungary are protected.

Follow the Hungarian countryside code: stay on the waymarked paths; do not light fires; keep dogs on a leash; do not play radios, pick flowers or leave litter; and camp only in designated areas. If you are taking a very large group into a national park ask the relevant authority for permission.

Access

During the Communist period egalitarianism was the ideology if not always the practice, but there was at least an emphasis on access to the countryside for all. In reality, however, international frontiers or areas near military installations were out of bounds. Agreements between the countries of the Warsaw Pact to control the movement of dissidents obliged the Hungarians to patrol the border with fellow socialist Czechoslovakia, and anyone who strayed too close to the frontier was escorted away at gunpoint, or worse. Today the problem for walking access is privatisation. Although Hungarian law obliges private landowners to honour waymarked routes set up before privatisation there have been problems such as landowners building fences without consultation. The main pressure group dealing with walkers' access issues, the Union of the Hungarian Friends of Nature (MTSZ), was involved in government negotiations with private forest owners, but is powerless in the face of failed negotiations with other landowners.

With a few exceptions the walks described in the guide follow the official waymarked trails to ensure that there are no access problems or disputes with landowners. Apart from the restricted areas mentioned above it is permissible to explore the many unmarked tracks through state forest land and national parks. Hungarian walkers tend to follow waymarks, so this is a good way of seeing the more secretive wildlife such as the moufflon or eagle owl. Respect boundaries whether in the public or private domain: do not climb fences or gates unless there is a ladder provided and it is on a waymarked route. Appendix 2 lists a few warning and no entry signs the walker is likely to encounter. As a general rule stay out of an area with signs saying *Tilos!* or *Figyelem!*

VILLAGE FACILITIES

The practical information about accommodation and local public transport should cover the traveller's needs, but as much of the walking passes through villages it is worth mentioning a few points. A village with a tiny population can be spread along a very long main street – more than a mild inconvenience if you have walked a long way on a hot day. Facilities are often not well centralised, and it can be a long trek to find accommodation, a shop or a bar which is situated, from the exhausted walker's point of view, at the wrong end of the village. A few tourist-friendly villages have information boards in English and German but they are often poorly designed, badly translated or have faded lettering. With few exceptions village shops tend to close by midday Saturday and do not open again until Monday, although shops in villages geared to tourists open later and on Sundays. Bread runs out early, and good-quality fruit and vegetables are difficult to find because most villagers grow their own. Look out for tables in front of houses laden with garden produce. There is an honesty box for the payment, although it is not often clear how much the householders, who are rarely around, want for a green pepper.

Every village has one or two bars called a *kocsma, italbolt, söröző* or *eszpresszó,* which is usually a very basic affair, full of men, and often does not have a women's toilet, but despite this they are not hostile places for women. When entering a bar it is proper to greet the occupants with the polite address. If you are a man do not be surprised if locals coming into the bar shake everyone's hand including yours before going up to order a drink. Some villages have a restaurant geared to the tourist trade offering excellent dishes made from locally caught game. Menus often have English and German translations.

Camera film is rarely available in the countryside, but try the post office, where postcards and maps are also on sale. For walking and camping gear Budapest and Miskolc have several shops which stock a variety of camping stove gas canisters and insect repellent (see Appendix 4).

Most villages run an annual fair (*búcsú*) or folk festival (*falunapok*) which celebrates the wine harvest or the end of winter. The festival may involve a church procession, outdoor concerts, marching bands, and women in regional costume. There are also less traditional music festivals and art days set in pretty regions such as the Káli-medence in the Balaton Uplands or the Zemplén. Check with the local branch of Tourinform for details of any festivals in the area. Many villages have a tiny museum of local life and traditions, or *tájház*. Unfortunately the museum is often locked, although the curator can be contacted at the address on the fence or in the window. Locals are usually helpful and if they spot a tourist lurking around the museum they will pass the message on to the curator who probably lives in the village. Museums are closed on Mondays.

It is rare to find public conveniences in villages, and the toilet for the bar is probably a very primitive affair such as a shed around the back. Things are set to improve, and cafés often have very good facilities. Toilets in the rail and bus stations of small towns are often in a poor condition and have no toilet paper unless there is an attendant to whom you pay a few *forints*. Look for the universal WC sign or *Mosdó,* and if there is no male or female symbol on the WC door *Férfi* is man and *Női* woman.

FLORA, FUNGI AND FAUNA

The actions of thermal springs and karst drainage have created today's landscape of deep wooded valleys, montane beech forest, damp gullies, caves, sink-holes, sun-bleached limestone outcrops, upland meadows and rolling downland, providing habitats for a variety of rare and endangered plants. Hungary's vegetation zones range from Carpathian in the northern hills to Mediterranean in the south, but there are

Monkshood on Csóványos, Börzsöny, Walk 4

also pockets of sub-alpine, Illyrian and Boreal species which are relicts from the Ice Age. The basalt crags in the Balaton region provide a micro-climate for the lip fern, a survivor of warmer times, and the open karst and volcanic outcrops harbour several species of stonecrop and saxifrage. In the sinkholes of the Bükk-fennsík plateau temperatures have been recorded well below freezing on a summer night, creating a unique habitat for the aconite, gentian, carline thistle and Austrian dragonshead. Hungary's position in east-central Europe and touching on the Balkan peninsula encourages forest to grow at high altitudes. Beech, hornbeam and oak are the commonest species, although there are many varieties of fruit trees and bushes specific to Hungary.

There are almost 500 types of mushroom in Hungary, and woodland species of the boletus, russula and inocybe groups are commonly found. In the early nineteenth century the German settlers in the Bakony collected bracket fungus for tinder to light pipes and make hats. Today mushroom-foraging continues to play a small part in village economies.

The relatively undisturbed forests are a haven for wild game such as roe deer, red deer and, less commonly, the moufflon, introduced from Corsica in the 1920s. The wild boar is largely nocturnal, and the walker is more likely to see the upturned turf of its foraging than the animal itself. Red squirrel, pine marten, badger and fox are also present, but the wildcat, which prefers old beech forest, is very shy. Hungary's hundreds of caves and crevices have attracted speleologists and archaeologists from all over the world, but also provide a good habitat for many species of bat, including the Mediterranean Horseshoe Bat. Lynx and wolf were once extinct, but thanks to a hunting ban since the 1970s have been making a cautious comeback in the Aggtelek and Zemplén. The brown bear is a very rare visitor from Slovakia.

Birdwatchers coming to Hungary tend to concentrate on Hungary's wetlands and the Great Plain, but the highlands also offer plenty of interest. It is worth taking a pair of 8x40 binoculars to sort out the various species of raptor wheeling over forest meadows. Rare but on the increase, the Saker falcon can be seen on the high Bükk plateau, and the range of the imperial eagle is spreading thanks to conservation efforts. Several species of owl seem to have survived the days when superstitious villagers killed them, and the remoter parts of the northern forests provide a habitat for the eagle owl. North-east Hungary is also at the western limit of the ural owl. There are many species of woodpecker, including the black woodpecker with its unmistakable

Salamander, Oltár-patak, Börzsöny, Walk 4

plaintive call. The rare hazelhen, a woodland-loving member of the grouse family, is also to be found in the north. Orchards, smallholdings, vineyards and downs provide breeding sites for summer visitors such as the golden oriole, wryneck, hoopoe and many species of warbler. Thorny scrub on heaths and farmland provides a grisly larder for shrikes, and a closer look at sandbanks in open country and farmland will reveal colonies of hole-nesting bee-eaters. Stony hillsides are the haunt of rock buntings, stonechats and ravens. Overgrown damp meadows with scattered bushes are the haunt of the shy corncrake. White storks nest on village chimney pots and pylons in a few villages in the hills, but the black stork also breeds in small numbers in the north.

The hills have a variety of habitats suited to reptiles and amphibians. The lidless skink and sand lizard favour the sun-warmed rocks along the trails, and frogs breed precariously in shallow forest pools and flooded ruts of tracks. The spectacularly marked fire salamander can be spotted in the leaf litter along cool wooded stream banks. Despite the depredations of snake-skin hunters over the years, the common viper and other species continue to thrive.

Upland meadows are notable for many species of butterfly such as the beautiful swallowtail. The

37

25cm carpathian blue slug inhabits the Zemplén, and the black snail, an Ice Age relict, can be found along the old mill streams of the Bükkalja. In summer expect to see many species of longhorn beetle and the rather odd spectacle of stag beetles in flight.

HISTORY

Hungary's highlands are peripheral to Hungarian life today, but they were once the scene of competing empires, faiths and ideologies, and have played a large part in the struggles for national liberation. Settlement in the hills began long before recorded time, and excavations of Hungary's many caves have provided evidence that the highlands were inhabited about half a million years ago. The region has been notable as a crossing point for the great migrations, and the first important groups were the Bronze Age Illyrians and Thracians, who migrated north from the Balkans into the Carpathian Basin. They built hill forts to defend themselves from another incomer, the northern Celts, who eventually dominated the region. By AD 100 the Romans had defeated the Celts and created the province of Pannonia in the lands west of the Danube. To defend this eastern frontier of the Empire the Romans built a line of fortifications (*limes*) stretching from the Mecsek to the Danube Bend and deployed Syrian

light cavalry against the Sarmatians and Germans.

By the end of the fourth century AD the elite of Rome had retreated, leaving a partly urbanised population practising viticulture and Christianity. Germanic tribes swept south to exploit the power vacuum, but in turn were defeated by Attila the Hun, who harried settlements as far west as the Rhine. After the Huns came Teutonic Longobards, proto-Slavs and Turkic-Bulgars, but they were held in check by another nomadic people from the East, the Avars, who for 250 years ruled over a multi-ethnic empire anticipating the shape of modern-day Hungary.

In the ninth century the Carpathian Basin was divided between the Moravian and East Frankish empires. Large areas of the disputed marches were sparsely populated, and in the year 896 there was little resistance when the Magyar chieftan Árpád led the ancestors of the Hungarians into the Carpathian Basin. In 906 they destroyed the Moravian Empire and in 907, after defeating Gemanic tribes, occupied Pannonia. In the manner of the Huns before them the Magyars used the region as a base to raid for booty and slaves, and their forays, as far afield as France and Spain, prompted the western prayer: *From the arrows of the Hungarians, save us Lord.*

The turning point for Hungarian history was the year 955 at the Battle of Augsburg, when Emperor Otto I defeated the Magyar light cavalry forcing the fledgling Hungarian state to align itself with Western Europe. In 972, Géza, great-grandson of Árpád, converted to Christianity, and in 1001 István was crowned with papal approval and laid the foundations of the Hungarian state.

In 1241 the Mongols swept through Hungary and defeated the Hungarian army at the Battle of Muhi. King Béla IV and the remnants of his shattered army retreated through the hills of the Bükk and sought refuge on the Dalmatian coast. There was famine and epidemic, but on his return Béla ordered the building of stone castles to replace the hilltop stockades. The Mongols did not return, but during the fifteenth century the castles served as strongholds for Hussite rebels.

It was King Matthias who drove the Hussites out of the northern hills. The rule of this clever king is considered to be Hungary's Golden Age, but he was also an expansionist, and with the help of a mercenary army ruled an enlarged kingdom stretching, for a while at least, from the Mediterranean to the Baltic. After his death, Hungary was weakened by a succession crisis and a failed peasant uprising and fell easily to Suleiman the Magnificent at the Battle of Mohács in 1526. For 150 years Hungary was divided between the Austrian and Ottoman empires, and during intermittent periods of warfare the hilltop strongholds frequently changed hands. The defeat of the Ottomans at the end of the seventeenth century was followed by Hungarian uprisings against the Habsburg occupation, and for a while the rebels held much of the country and dominated the northern hills. After their defeat the lands of the rebellious nobles were confiscated. German and Slovak Catholics and other ethnic groups were settled in the hills to manage the forests, run the glass foundries and also stem the advance of the Reformation. Those hilltop castles still standing lost strategic importance, and for a while the highlands no longer played a large part in Hungary's history.

After World War I the price of fighting and losing on the Austrian side was the loss of two-thirds of Hungary's lands. Important industry was lost and three million Hungarians ended up in foreign territory. During World War II Hungary joined the Axis powers, and as a reward received some of the territory it had lost, but once again a dangerous combination of inept diplomacy, internal weakness and unfortunate geography transformed Hungary and its hills into a battleground for foreign armies. Recalling the Habsburg–Ottoman

Walking on Nagy-Mána, Börzsöny, Walk 5

wars the Zemplén, Bükk, Vértes, Bakony and Pilis became battle fronts.

After the war the Hungarian Socialist Workers Party eased itself into power and Hungary became a one-party state and ally of the Soviet Union. At the same time the ethnic composition of the hill villages was radically altered as large numbers of the original German and Slovak settlers were forcibly resettled and smallholders came under pressure to give up their land and join the agricultural co-operatives or work in the cities. The drama of the 1956 Revolution, when Hungarians rebelled against the Communist government and its Soviet backers, was largely an urban affair, but the conflict in Pécs

spread into the Mecsek hills. Show trials, detentions, executions and mass emigration followed.

The death of Stalin and the consolidation of the post-1956 Communist state gave the new regime under János Kádár freedom for manoeuvre. Living standards improved, and from 1968 there was a good deal of political and economic liberalisation with experiments in privatisation. This softer brand of state socialism was jokingly referred to as 'goulash communism'. In the 1980s the Soviet Empire unravelled, and Hungary played a large part in the opening up of the border between East and West. Hungary's transition from a one-party state to a mixed-economy democracy was relatively smooth and peaceful, although there has been a social cost for hill villagers who had depended on agricultural co-operatives or mining for their livelihood.

VILLAGE LIFE

Without playing down the bitterness felt by better-off smallholders who were forced to collectivise, agricultural co-operatives were often very successful enterprises with profitable spin-off activities. Villagers were guaranteed work in the co-operatives or in the nearby factories and mines. After the petty restrictions of the 1950s were lifted many householders had the opportunity to grow their own produce and rear livestock with fodder provided free by the co-operative. There were other positive aspects such as weekly voluntary work commitment (*társadalmi munka*) involving community projects. Village children were also deployed to collect litter and clear streams.

The changes after 1989 saw many co-operatives disband and villagers gain more land to work as private holdings, but today unemployment is high in hill regions such as the Bükk, Zemplén and Mecsek. The pull of vibrant and cosmopolitan Budapest has exacerbated the problem of rural depopulation started during the Communist period. Impossibly neat peasant houses, manicured lawns and no barking dogs is usually a sign,

however charming at first glance, that you are passing through a village where most inhabitants have died out and the cottages are now holiday homes.

In Budapest streets and squares have been renamed and statues removed in an attempt to erase the memory of the Communist era, but many village communities have neither the resources nor the inclination to indulge in symbolic acts. As a result many of the old street names continue to exist: Béke utca (Peace Street); Felszabadulás utca (Liberation Street); Vörös Hadsereg utca (Red Army Street); not to mention Lenin utca.

A HISTORY OF HUNGARY'S WALKING MOVEMENTS

It is a mistake to view the development of recreational walking in Hungary as a harmless pastime detached from history. The growth of walking clubs followed the same pattern as the rest of Europe, members of the professional classes, who had more leisure time, taking the lead. Hungary's first club, Magyarországi Kárpát Egyesület (MKE), Hungarian Carpathian Association, was founded in 1873 and it played a major role in the exploration of the Tatras. During the 1880s its Budapest section decided to explore the Pilis and in 1891 seceded from the MKE and set up the Magyar Turista Egyesület

(MTE), Hungarian Association of Walkers. During its first two years its members had waymarked 240km (148 miles) of trails, built refuges, cleared wells and springs, and founded a magazine, *Turisták Lapja*. The first of the working-class clubs, the Munkás Testedzők Turista Egyesülete (MTTE), Hungarian Workers' Sport Walkers Association, was set up in 1908. A group of printers created the Természetbarátok Turista Egyesülete (TTE), Association of the Friends of Nature, in 1910, and another important working-class club, the Magyar Turista Szövetsége (MTSZ), Union of Hungarian Walkers, was founded in 1913. Over the next 20 years there were other clubs, adding to the confusion of acronyms. Their aim was to promote class-consciousness, healthy living and temperance, and they maintained links with the Austrian Natur Freund clubs and the wider social democratic movement. Inevitably the political affiliations of many walking clubs led to splits and mergers. After much bitter infighting the MKE, MTE and TTE merged under the MTSZ. At the Treaty of Trianon after World War I, Hungary lost the Tatras to Czechoslovakia, but as if to compensate the walking movement in Hungary expanded. Ideology continued to play a part and many clubs were aligned with rightist or leftist causes.

The growth of independent walking movements ceased in 1944 when the Germans deposed the Regent, Miklós Horthy, and handed power to the Hungarian Fascist party, the Arrow Cross. After the war the Communist regime disbanded all the pre-war walking clubs whether 'bourgeois', rightist (some clubs had had members active in the Arrow Cross) or socialist. A new organisation, the Magyar Természetbarát Szövetség (Union of the Hungarian Friends of Nature), was set up on the Soviet model in 1949. To add to the confusion (or perhaps encourage the idea that the new organisation was a continuation of the more politically acceptable pre-Communist Union of Hungarian Walkers with the same acronym), the Friends of Nature organisation was called the MTSZ.

Between the wars about 50 walking hostels had been built by the efforts of members of various walking clubs, but when the Communists gained power they were collectivised. This was a particularly bitter blow to the members of the disbanded working-class clubs who had struggled hard to find the resources to build the hostels. Unfortunately the state tourist agency had no long-term interest in the buildings and many hostels were neglected. In 1974 the state allocated the buildings to catering and tourism enterprises for the purpose of making a profit, but many were allowed to decay until they were unsafe and had to be demolished.

In 1987 the MTSZ became independent of the state and in 1990, a little over a hundred years after its foundation, the MTE was re-formed. Since the political transition of the late 1980s walking has, according to some Hungarians, declined, although masochistic challenge walks modelled on the Czech tradition have become popular. By the end of the twentieth century a new generation not burdened by history or ideology was taking up walking, and walking club membership was rising.

THE NATIONAL BLUE ROUTE

In 1938 the MTSZ set up Hungary's first long-distance walk, the Szent István-túra (Saint Stephen's Way). The 852km (526 mile) route started at Tapolca in the Balaton region and finished at Tokaj-hegy, the southernmost hill of the Zemplén. Its first chairman was Jenő Cholnoky, the revisionist geographer who bitterly opposed the redrawing of Hungary's borders at the Treaty of Trianon. After World War II the route fell into disuse, but during the 1950s the Budapest railway workers' union revived it. At first the route was managed by and for the exclusive use of railway workers. The union produced a guidebook and

Regéc Castle, Zemplén, Walk 17

introduced a badge scheme for walkers who completed the whole distance. In 1961 it was taken over by the Communist MTSZ, whose members founded the 'Blue Route Movement', a campaign to lengthen the original Saint Stephen's Way. This led to the creation of the Országos Kéktúra (National Blue Route), which crossed the length of Hungary starting at Nagy-Milic on the Czechoslovakian border in the east and finishing at Írott-kő on the Austrian border. Considering the sensitivity of these frontiers during the Cold War it was quite an achievement. The MTSZ installed stamping points along the various stages of the route (they can still be seen today) and a certificate was issued to walkers who completed all 1093km (675 miles).

In the early 1980s Pál Rockenbauer walked the National Blue Route with a film crew and the outcome was the very popular television documentary *One Million Steps Around Hungary*. Rockenbauer took the opportunity to highlight the unavailability of basic walking gear and the lack of budget accommodation along the route for walkers. He was also exasperated by signs of rural decline such as vandalism, litter, the depopulation of villages due to the Communist government's centralisation policies, and insensitive planning by local authorities.

The political changes in 1988 prompted the MTSZ to suggest a commemoration walk for the 950th anniversary of Saint Stephen's death and the fiftieth anniversary of the Saint Stephen's Way. The event was approved and the frontier controls relaxed in order for the two groups of walkers to start at different ends and meet at the middle in Dobogókő as their predecessors had done in 1938.

In 1995 the National Blue Route was officially connected to the E3, the pan-European long-distance path linking Spain with Turkey. Unfortunately the link is broken at the Austrian and Slovakian borders, where it is necessary to come off route and use an official border crossing via the main road. A few Hungarians do walk the entire National Blue Route, which also crosses the Great Plain, and have the badge to prove it. Many of the stages linking the hill ranges can be boring or involve lengthy road bashing, but if you are interested, contact the headquarters of the MTSZ (see Appendix 4) or visit the Cartographia map shop to obtain a copy of the official booklet, *Országos Kéktúra: Útvonalvázlat és Igazoló Füzet*. It has spaces to stamp the stages, but take your own inkpad as the ones at the stamping points dry out. Cartographia also publishes *Országos Kéktúra*, an illustrated guide to the whole route. The text is in Hungarian, but its 1:40 000 maps are invaluable for their coverage of all the stages.

WALKS IN
NORTHERN HUNGARY

The Aggtelek

After the Treaty of Trianon, when Hungary's borders
were redrawn, Jenő Cholnoky, the Hungarian geographer, condemned the outcome as 'a geographical
absurdity, which history will deservedly condemn'.
Without adding weight to revisionist claims, the
Slovak-Hungarian border, which divides the Gömör-
Torna karst in two, is at the very least a geological
absurdity. Millions of years ago the hills on both sides
of today's frontier began as sediments covered in a
tropical sea. After the water receded, the exposed
limestone was eroded, creating a landscape of karst
forest, alpine meadows, sink-holes and dolinas. The
social and political consequences of the redrawing of
Hungary's borders are still being played out, but the
national park authorities in both Slovakia and
Hungary have risen above it to co-operate in order to
protect this unique region. For an idea of the extent
of the whole karst buy the 1:50 000 map Aggteleki
Nemzeti Park/Slovenský Kras (published by Paulus),
available at the Aggtelek and Jósvafő visitor centres
and bookshops in Budapest.

Hungary's share of the Gömör-Torna region, the
Aggteleki-karszt, lies 155km (95 miles) north-east of
Budapest. The Aggtelek is a low-lying range and its
highest summit, Fertős-tető, is 604m (1981ft) high,
but a good view can be had from the 461m (1512ft)
hilltop fortress ruin of Szád-vár in Ménes-völgy. A
common feature of the range is red soil, evidence of
iron-ore deposits created by the actions of hot
springs in Triassic times. Thermal activity is ever
present, and the water gushing out of the cave above
Jósvafő maintains a constant temperature of 15°C
(59°F). Beneath the forested hills and meadows lies
the Baradla cave system of 276 caves, which is one of

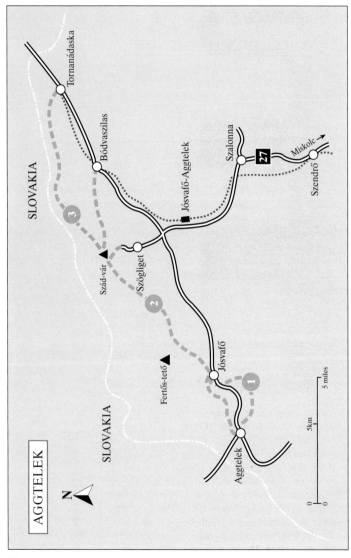

Szád-vár,
Aggtelek, Walk 2

the most complex in Europe. One of the largest caves, the Óriások Terme (Great Hall), has an impressive collection of stalactites and stalagmites. The system is now a UNESCO World Heritage site and the caves attract visitors ranging from curious tourists to serious pot-holers. There are public access entrances in the villages of Aggtelek, Jósvafő and the pond called Vörös-tó, and one on the Slovakian side at Domica. Guided cave tours depart at regular intervals and are graded according to difficulty and length. The more demanding excursions require special equipment and pot-holing experience. Wear warm clothing to visit the caves; on a hot summer day the sudden drop from 35°C (95°F) to 10°C (50°F) can be quite a shock.

History
When the Magyars came to this corner of Hungary they brought the Kavars, a nomadic tribe of Khazars, and many place-names can be attributed to this Turkic-speaking people. The region has a long history of mineral extraction: German and Slav tribes dug out the iron ore and in the nineteenth century a demand for agricultural implements revived these old metal-working traditions. The Tengerszem pond is a favourite spot for family picnics, but it was constructed to feed the mill race for the water mill in Jósvafő. The soil is not very good, but fine wine was produced here until the nineteenth-century Phyloxera epidemic. The legacy of Aggtelek's viticulture is a nearby hill called Szőlőhegy (Vineyard Hill).

The Aggtelek is as battle-weary as any part of highland Hungary and has been invaded and occupied by Hussites, Ottomans and Austrians. There was no let-up for the locals during the twentieth century. In response to Hungary's invasion to regain its territorial losses after World War I, the Czechs launched a counter-invasion, and during World War II the region became an arena for the struggle between the German and Russian armies, forcing villagers to seek refuge in the Baradla caves.

Routes
Most visitors to the Aggtelek come to see the caves, and subsequently the trails, which tend to follow the Hungarian-Slovak border, are often empty. A combination of infrequent use, convoluted trails and poor waymarking in the Vecsem-bükk heights of the northeast can lead the walker into Slovakia by accident. During Communism the Aggtelek was a favourite place for clandestine border crossings and it is still

illegal to cross into Slovakia this way. Red and white concrete pillars along a firebreak mark the frontier, so there should be no excuse for wandering into Slovakia by accident. Elsewhere waymarking is generally good, although there is some confusion around the approach to Szád-vár castle ruin. From the point of view of navigation Cartographia's Aggtelek map has an unhelpful design: the north-eastern end of the range is placed in an inset box at the bottom of the map. However, there is a very useful and interesting 1:20 000 inset of the Aggtelek–Jósvafő area and cave network. The Aggtelek is an important nature reserve and many areas are out of bounds; keep to the waymarked routes.

Transport

Two buses a day go direct to Jósvafő and Aggtelek from Budapest Népstadion and there is an extra service on weekends for Tornanádaska. Getting there by train is a bit more complicated: at Budapest Keleti get on the fastest service to Miskolc and then take the local train on the Tornanádaska line. Walk-in points at Jósvafő and Aggtelek are about 16km (10 miles) from Jósvafő–Aggtelek railway halt, but local bus services are integrated with the train timetable.

Accommodation

The Aggtelek is geared up for foreign tourists and the national park publishes two excellent English-language booklets: *The Caves of the Aggtelek Karst* and *Event and Service Guide to the Aggtelek National Park*. The latter is updated yearly and includes information about local geology, history, cave tour schedules and eco-tours, and has a list of accommodation in the area. The booklet is available at the national park gift shops at the Aggtelek cave entrance and in Jósvafő, at the cave tour booking office and the Tengerszem Hotel. As a base Jósvafő is the most pleasant village, but its rooms are likely to be booked up in summer. Aggtelek village has many rooms, concentrated mainly on Ady Endre utca, although it is worth looking around for other options. The camping complex and national park centre clustered around the Aggtelek cave entrance is less than 2km (about a mile) from the village itself and has a hostel, wooden chalets for hire and plenty of camping spaces with full facilities including a restaurant. Make enquiries at the *Recepció* of the Barlang-szálló. The Gömör-Torna Festival in late July is likely to increase pressure on bed space.

Points of interest in the Aggtelek

Aggtelek village

It is a miracle that the fourteenth-century settlement of Ogh-teluk has survived to the present day. The village has endured invading Hussites, Ottomans and Poles; the Plague and cholera; and in 1858 it had to be rebuilt after a fire. In 1919 the Czech army invaded, and in World War II the Russians pounded it with Katyusha rockets. The bell tower on the main street was originally a watchtower built by either the Hussites or Ottomans, but the ornate facings and bell were added in 1802. The tablets on the tower list the villagers who died in the two world wars. The inscription reads: *They never returned from the blood storm of World War II.*

Bódvaszilas

This was a thriving village until the Hussites plundered the region. It was also renowned for sheep, and in the late nineteenth century marble quarrying was important.

Borókás töbrök

The information board describes how the juniper-dotted landscape of dolinas (*töbrök*) is in the first stage of reforestation.

Derenk

This scattering of ruins was once a thriving village with about a hundred families who made a living as smallholders, foresters, charcoal-burners and tinsmiths. In 1940 the Hungarian parliament passed a law to resettle its inhabitants so that Admiral Miklós Horthy, Regent of Hungary, could turn the area into a bear-hunting reserve. The largest building still standing was the school. The villagers were relocated to Emőd on the plain, and on All Saints' Day their descendants come back to eat goulash among the ruins and say prayers for the dead.

Jewish cemetery

On the other side of the cemetery hill is a reminder of the often forgotten Jewish presence in rural Hungary. Many Jews were smallholders and others brought technical innovations to the countryside. In 1840, the Klein family built a water mill and iron foundry in Jósvafő. During World War II Jósvafő's Jews, like so many, were deported never to return.

Jósvafő

Slav tribes first settled this valley and built an earth fort. In the Middle Ages Teutonic knights converted it into a monastery, but there is no trace of it today. The bell tower was originally a look-out and probably built by Hussites. During the 1848–49 Revolution Austrian troops passed through the village after the Battle of Branyiszko. Today the population is less than 400, but the villagers maintain a collective spirit. The museum has an impressive collection of nineteenth-century iron-smelting equipment as well as an exhibition about the history of the exploration of Baradla caves. The museum provides an English-language information card explaining the exhibits and local history.

Kőnyerő hely

A former quarry, this is where villagers once dug for iron-free limestone. There are fossils in the rock, and this is also the only place in the Aggtelek National Park where it is permitted to remove rock samples.

Protestant cemetery

The wooden grave posts in Jósvafő cemetery first appeared at the end of the Ottoman Empire when followers of the Reformation wished to distinguish their memorials from those of Roman Catholics. Posts are often in husband and wife pairs. The carvings are not arbitrary: a star represents a man; tulips, weeping willow or rosemary, a woman; and a tulip for a child. The cast-iron memorial near the top of the hill is of Slovakian origin and marks the grave of a Protestant minister. Inscriptions on many grave posts express disappointment and bitterness:

> *Here I lie. I lived 75 years.*
> *There is so much suffering in the world*
> *And I had my fair share of it.*
> *Farewell and God be with you!*

Szád-vár

The substantial ruins still standing give a good feel for the size of this thirteenth-century castle built to guard the route along which minerals extracted from the local mines were transported. In the fifteenth century the Hussites occupied the fort and in 1556 Zsófia Patócsi, the lady of the castle, successfully withstood an Austrian siege while her husband was absent. Hungarian rebels of the first uprising against Habsburg rule held it in 1644 and 1682, but in 1686 the castle was destroyed.

Szelcepuszta-völgy

A herd of *hucul* horses can be seen grazing on the broad meadow of the valley. This unique gene pool is maintained by the Aggtelek National Park and many of the horse-related place-names such as Lófej (Horse Head), Ménes (Horse Herd) and Patkós (Horseshoe) have not changed for centuries, suggesting that the early Magyars brought the breed from Central Asia. Szelcepuszta at the north end of the valley was the hunting lodge of Admiral Miklós Horthy. Accommodation at the forest lodge passed on the way is only available if pre-booked.

Tó-hegy

The information board on Tó-hegy explains that the open karst meadow (*nyílt karrmező*) is a product of deforestation caused by forest fires and centuries of overgrazing. Water, acids and micro-organisms have carved the rocks into bizarre formations prompting the local name for the meadow, Ördögszántás (Devil's Field). The pond at the bottom of the hill is a sink-hole and was the village cabbage patch before it filled with water.

Tornanádaska

Above the village there is a ruined medieval castle obscured by the eighteenth-century mansion house. In the nineteenth century it was fashionable for the Hungarian aristocracy to create English-style parks. The mansion gardens were created over many years by covering the karst in a layer of imported soil. Over 200 species were planted. The building is now an institute for children and private property.

Vecsem-bükki-zsomboly

The Aggtelek karst has hundreds of pot-holes, dolinas and sink-holes, but this example is one of the deepest. Beneath the sealed entrance the shaft drops a further 245m (803ft).

Vörös-tó

It is no more than an overgrown pond now, but the name (Red Lake) is a reference to the colour of the soil in the region formed over 50 million years ago. Up to the left of the pond is the Medve-sziklák (Bear Rocks) formed from limestone during the Cretaceous Period.

Zomboly-lyuk víznyelő

This is a sink-hole which drains water into the Baradla cave system below.

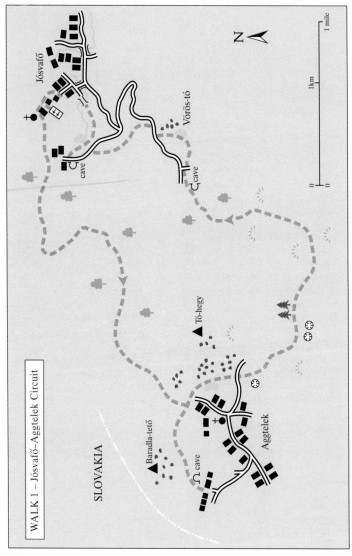

WALK 1 – Jósvafő-Aggtelek Circuit

Jósvafő

Vörös-tó

cave

C cave

Tó-hegy

Baradla-tető

Ω cave

Aggtelek

SLOVAKIA

N

1km

1 mile

0

0

WALK 1
Jósvafő–Aggtelek Circuit

Route:	Jósvafő – Tó-hegy – Aggtelek
Distance:	12km (7.5 miles)
Map:	1 Aggteleki-karszt és környékének 1:40 000
Transport:	Regular buses between Aggtelek and Jósvafő
Refreshments:	There are restaurants and snack bars around the Jósvafő and Aggtelek cave entrances but the prices in the village bars are better. There is a cheap and friendly canteen at the back of the pub in Jósvafő village proper where the locals eat. Find the little passage on the right of the bar leading to the door.

There are two ways to walk between the villages of Jósvafő and Aggtelek. One is via the Baradla cave, and if this is your preferred route contact the booking office above Jósvafő near the Tengerszem Hotel for details of the five-hour guided tour through a labyrinth of stalagmites and stalactites. Otherwise the overground route is a pleasant walk through forested hills and over some typical karst landscape. The walking also follows a geological study trail (*tanösvény út*) with a series of yellow information boards marking places of interest along the way. The waymarking is fine through the forest section on the approach to Aggtelek village, but the return to Jósvafő over meadow and karst requires concentration. When waymarks are missing on tree-less meadow, wooden posts with a white flash signify a turning. The route description assumes the walker is starting at Jósvafő but the circular nature of the walk allows an Aggtelek start.

Starting at central **Jósvafő** at the bar turn right and follow the main street over the bridge. As the street bends left take the second street right over a smaller bridge. On the other side turn right to follow the street along the stream for a few paces and then turn left up the little road passing between the recently renovated water mill and the village museum (*Tájház*). Veer right, passing the traditional Palóc style cottage (the oldest house in the village) and continue uphill past the bell tower and the footpath up to the **Protestant cemetery**. Continue straight towards the wall of the Protestant church and turn left up a narrow path with blue waymarks through the trees until the wooden arch of the forlorn little **Jewish cemetery**. Head diagonally left across the grass and pick up a little path through the woods to a wider track. To stay on the blue waymarks turn right and at the next fork keep left passing a small waterworks. The track eventually meets the green route coming up from the Tengerszem Hotel visible below. Continue on the Blue Route as it contours right. The blue-waymarked path meanders through mature forest gradually gaining height to reach a saddle and little clearing. Ignore the blue (triangle) turning for the summit of Baradla-tető on the right; the top is over-

Tó-hegy karst

grown. The descent down the other side of the saddle brings the route out of the woods and to a meadow where the grassy track forks. ▶

At the fork of grassy tracks in the meadow take the left track which descends gently down to a fence. Aggtelek village is visible straight ahead but turn left to follow the yellow-waymarked path along the layered fence. For a short cut to the village and refreshments continue along the fence until the path swings right past old houses and climbs a steep rough street up to the main square and the village bar. Otherwise press on and pick up the yellow waymarks rising left past walnut trees and up the karst slope of **Tó-hegy**. Climb no higher than the information board before turning right. The waymarks, now painted on rocks, thin out but try to keep to the indistinct footpath. If the path is lost continue to contour until the trail picks up again, eventually traversing down through the bleached stones to the little pond at the back of the village. Follow the pond edge until the trail rises to a slip road with another information board.

Cross the main road and turn right for **Aggtelek village** and refreshments or, to continue with the return route to Jósvafő, cross straight over the main road and pick up the little path dropping down the other side into the depression of **Zomboly-lyuk víznyelő**. The grassy track passing vegetable plots is obvious for a while but peters out as it begins to traverse up the hill to the left. There are no waymarks in this open country but a stake with a white patch guides the route as it contours some bushes. If the main road is reached you have climbed too far. Try to find the beginning of a track dropping steeply down through a grove of fruit trees and bushes. At the bottom where it comes out of the trees and joins a more significant track turn to pass through meadow with scattered bushes. At the next fork keep left, and continue on the track across the meadows.

When the route splits into yellow and yellow (+) branches it is not very obvious but a white-flashed

Alternative Route
For a direct route to the Aggtelek cave entrance and campsite take the right branch of the fork. The track narrows to a footpath contouring a hillside with scattered juniper bushes and rocks. Visible down to the left are the karst slope on Tó-hegy and Aggtelek village. The blue and yellow waymarks take the route around a hill rising a little and then dropping down to the look-out point above the Aggtelek cave entrance. Turn right and the trail eventually picks up the concrete steps and walkway leading down to the tourist complex.

post marks a left turn down along a trail flanked by electricity pylons. An embankment with red soil and exposed chunks of limestone, **Kőnyerő hely**, is reached. Continue straight uphill towards a little saddle guided by the electricity pylons. The red soil of a path appears ahead as it climbs up through a patch of woods. On the other side veer right on the trail dropping down to a landscape of sink-holes, meadow and scattered juniper. The Hungarian for this landscape is **borókás töbrök**. The path soon joins the red gash of a track cutting through the rough grassland and scrub. Follow it as it swings left but do not continue all the way back up to the main road. Again, the waymarks are unhelpful, but a white-flashed post marks the point where the route turns away from the track and heads for the woods on the right. Once in the trees there is a good trail with yellow waymarks passing an information board listing the flora and fauna of the region. The walkway to the Vörös-tó cave entrance appears down on the right and eventually there is another information board. Join the asphalt cave access road and continue up to the junction. The main road is up to the left, but turn right for a few paces and turn left indicated by the yellow waymark on the concrete post. Pick up the path as it drops steeply down through bushes and over rough grassland to pass a reed-clogged pond called **Vörös-tó**.

After the pond the path becomes a rough track. At the rain hut turn left to gain the main road and follow it for a short while until the yellow waymarks indicate a path going left up the embankment back into the forest. The woodland trail with scattered rocks eventually descends back onto the road but veer away left to pick up a green route. Follow the forest trail and it will come out onto the Jósvafő cave approach road. Turn left for the cave entrance and the welcome sight of a restaurant. If continuing down to Jósvafő village, turn right to descend the steps to the car park and pick up the yellow trail through the

woods. After passing the Tengerszem pond stay on
the path along the stream, past a guesthouse, and
over a bridge into Jósvafő village.

WALK 2
Jósvafő to Bódvaszilas

Route:	Jósvafő – Szelce-völgy – Szád-vár – Bódvaszilas
Distance:	21km (13 miles)
Map:	1 Aggteleki-karszt és környékének 1:40 000
Transport:	To get back to Budapest there are trains and a limited bus service from Bódvaszilas to Miskolc.
Refreshments:	None on the way so take a packed lunch to eat on Szád-vár ruins. Bódvaszilas has a bar offering snacks, conveniently placed near the railway station.

A good track passes through the broad alpine meadows of Szelce-völgy. Sink-holes, herds of grazing
horses and the ruined village of Derenk with its
poignant story provide interest along the way. The
highlight of the walk is the view from the ruins of
Szád-vár castle set on a volcanic cone. A straightforward route for the first half of the walk, but the waymarking becomes erratic and quite confusing around
Szád-vár.

Start at **Jósvafő** village bar and head for the bridge
but do not cross; veer right on the village back road
following the stream. Leave the road on the second
right along a rough track rising up to the broad valley
and pastures of **Szelce-völgy**. There are no waymarks
but follow the obvious track straight ahead and
through the valley. The rocky slopes of Fertős-tető
rise up on the left. After about an hour the track
swings left through and along a fence and joins a
good road. Turn left to pass the Szelcepuszta Forest
Hostel. After the farm the road begins to swing left

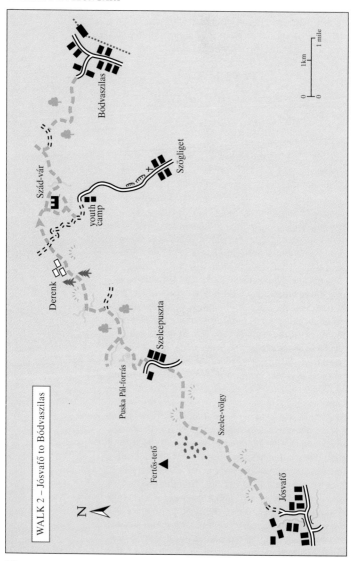

WALK 2 – Jósvafő to Bódvaszílas

N

Bódvaszílas

Szád-vár

Szögliget

youth camp

Derenk

Puska Pál-forrás

Szelcepuszta

Fertős-tető

Szelce-völgy

Jósvafő

1km
1 mile

for the old hunting lodge but leave it by veering right along a small path heading into woods.

Derenk village ruins

The path follows a high deer fence before becoming a forest track switching back on itself to descend the valley of Patkós-völgy and passes a spring called Puska Pál-forrás. The track levels at the bottom and joins a blue-waymarked track coming from the left. Join it and keep right to follow the stream. Soon after the track exits the forest, turn off at the next track left but do not go too far along it; look for the blue waymarks indicating a little path leaving to the right and climbing uphill through pine woods. The blue path crosses a track and climbs through another stand of forest to the top where there is a clearing with a junction of tracks. Head diagonally left for the overgrown track descending to a stream. At the bottom turn sharply right to cross the stream and follow the grassy track on the other side, switching back to rise gently over open pasture. There are no waymarks here but at a fork take the right trail through the pine woods. The trail soon exits the woodland to drop left swinging right along a broad flat-bottom valley to pass the ruins of **Derenk**.

After Derenk the track continues past a plantation and through open country with reed beds. Take
the next turning right to re-enter the woods, and soon
after the track joins a good road and a clearing. From
here Szád-vár's prominent cone is visible. Cross the
road and at the national park sign pick up the blue
waymarks for a rough trail across scrub and meadow.
The next path right descends into woodland. On the
way the foundations of an old lime-kiln are visible on
the left. At the next fork take the right branch out
onto a meadow and follow the overgrown path hug-
ging the forest edge. At the end of the path there are
trees. Turn right for the path climbing out of the
woods to peter out at a meadow on a saddle with a
conifer plantation on the right.

Ignore the waymarkings for the time being as
they are confusing. Continue straight ahead to cross
the meadow and head for the broadleaved woodland.
If the meadow is overgrown it might be easier to skirt
around the left side of the meadow. On the other side
there should be a track entering the forest. After a few
paces the first red (L) waymark should appear confirming the route. Where it joins another track, turn
left and uphill to swing around and up the castle hill
to the summit and the ruins of **Szád-vár**. ◀

To complete the whole route leave the fort and
retrace steps back down the same track and turn right
to regain the meadow on the saddle. Veer diagonally
right cutting across the meadow to pick up a rough and
overgrown track along the forest edge. After a few
paces turn off to the right to enter the woods. Look for
the red (L) waymarks and the vague trail veering right
to contour the hill, eventually passing the lower battlements of the castle ruin. As it descends the path disappears in places but the waymarks will guide the route
down. Cross the stream at the bottom and climb the
bank to the track with blue and red waymarks. Turn
right and then left to follow the blue waymarks up the
wooded valley called Bába-völgy. After five minutes
the little path climbs a steep bank and joins a broad

Quick Escape
After enjoying the
view from Szád-vár
do not go back to
the grassy saddle but
descend the winding
track all the way
down the hill. At the
bottom follow the
asphalt road left past
the youth camp and
continue to
Szögliget. Try not to
arrive late;
accommodation and
public transport are
limited in the village.

forest track. Follow this until it joins a red track swinging right and left over a spur. The rutted track descends the other side but do not follow it too far: look for a red-waymarked path leaving right and descending through the woods. At a level area near the bottom turn right to cross a clearing with scrub. The path veers left through bushes and from here gradually descends to a wide forest track with high banks. Follow it into **Bódvaszilas** and turn left along the main street for a bus stop or the railway station.

WALK 3
Tornanádaska to Szögliget

Route:	Tornanádaska – Vecsem-bükki-zsomboly – Szád-vár – Szögliget
Distance:	22km (13.5 miles)
Map:	1 Aggteleki-karszt és környékének 1:40 000
Transport:	Tornanádaska is a long way from Budapest and even the earliest train or bus will not get to the start until after midday. If depending on public transport arrange overnight accommodation in the area and start early the next day. From Szögliget there are a few bus services to Bódvaszilas for trains to Miskolc.
Refreshments:	None *en route*. Take a packed lunch or stock up at the little shop in Tornanádaska. There is a bar at Szögliget.

A different approach to Szád-vár castle ruin starting at the northern village of Tornanádaska. The winding terraced track zigzags up the karst slope – the only place in Europe where the Tornaian Golden Drop grows. For the most part good forest tracks wind through this lonely stretch of forest pitted with dozens of deep sink-holes. The climax is the walk up to the rambling ruins of Szád-vár fort and magnificent views down to the valley of Ménes-völgy. Waymarking is poor on the approach to Vecsem-bükk

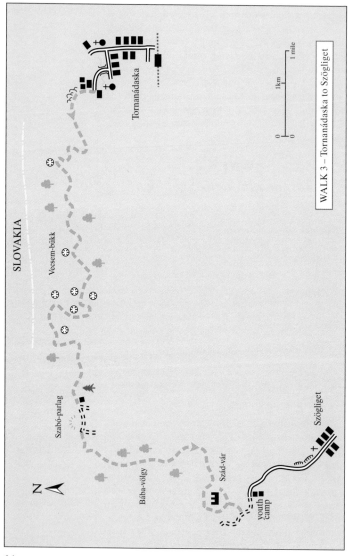

WALK 3 – Tornanádaska to Szögliget

and the convoluted yellow route involves a lot of guesswork. An early start will afford a leisurely walk and plenty of time to recover from navigation errors. This is a sensitive wildlife area; please do not stray from the path. The Slovakian frontier is only a hundred metres away at several points along the route. The section of map for the beginning of the route is awkwardly placed in an inset box at the bottom of the map.

From the station walk up to **Tornanádaska** church. The boundary for the children's hospital is straight ahead and on the left a little park with picnic tables. Turn left and follow the rough street almost as far as a little chapel. Turn right to cross the little bridge over the stream and veer left following the road past a row of houses. After the last village houses turn right into a field and follow the path rising gently to follow the perimeter of a youth camp. Ignore the first fork in the path and continue straight ahead and uphill through scrub but eventually bear left. After passing an old

View from Szád-vár

65

quarry the path becomes narrow and stony as it traverses the escarpment. Trees thin out and the path crosses bushy karst with views down to the Bódva Valley and soon begins its zigzagging climb. At the top of this first stage, woodland with storm-felled trees lies straight ahead. Pick up the yellow waymarks to ascend a wooded slope. At a clearing there is a steep drop-away ahead – the first of the sink-holes called Pasnyak-töbör. Veer left away from it and pass through conifers to pick up the narrow overgrown path traversing uphill.

The path contours the hill through an area of scattered juniper trees and conifers. At the top there is more open karst; at the grassy track turn right. The track begins to narrow to a trail winding around an area with scattered trees and between two large sink-holes. The waymarking on the Vecsem-bükk is poor but continue straight ahead and the trail gains more height before veering right. From here the route is overgrown and waymarks a rare treat, but keep straight ahead on the most obvious trail. After passing an old stone shelter set in a sink-hole there is a clearing. Turn left, skirting around another deep sink-hole overgrown with trees, and as the path approaches a woodland edge veer right into the next stand of woodland.

Yellow waymarks begin to appear now and the path is better trod. It swings right and passes through mature forest rising gently to a T-junction with the blue (+) route. Turn right to descend the now obviously waymarked yellow route. Do not go too far; the route leaves this good track on a narrow path descending to the left – otherwise you will end up at the Slovak border. Follow the waymarks to arrive at the yellow (omega) waymarks and the diversion to the **Vecsem-bükki-zsomboly**.

Veer around to the left of the turn-off for the cave and continue downhill on a broad track. There are plenty of yellow waymarks as the track winds through the forest until a meadow called Szabó-parlag. Stay on the track as it cuts straight across the meadow to the other side and a crossroads of tracks. Continue straight ahead to join a well-rutted vehicle track and then turn right to pass a forester's house. The yellow route drops away to the left but continue on the well-used track straight ahead now on the blue waymarks. After an area of managed forest with well-maintained fences the track begins to swing left. As it does, drop down to the right on the blue-waymarked track for the valley of Bába-völgy.

It is a long descent but at the bottom of the valley the trail joins a track. Turn right and find the red-(L)-waymarked trail which crosses the stream and zigzags up and around the north-eastern side of Szád-vár hill. The faint trail levels off near the top to skirt around the lower battlements of the ruins. From here the waymarks are confusing because of a diversion but continue straight ahead until the path peters out at the edge of the forest. At the grassy meadow on a saddle boxed in by forest turn left following the woodland edge. At the other side turn at a right angle along the next edge and turn left at a track entering the forest. After a few paces the red (L) waymarks should reappear confirming the route. At the next track turn left to contour around and up to the ruins of **Szád-vár**.

To leave the fort retrace the steps to descend but ignore the turn-off back to the meadow. Continue to descend down the red (L) path to the bottom of the hill. At the road turn left to pass a youth camp, after which the well-surfaced road passes old quarries with information boards before coming to the first houses of Szögliget. Follow the long street lined with pear trees to a pub and turn left for the bus stop.

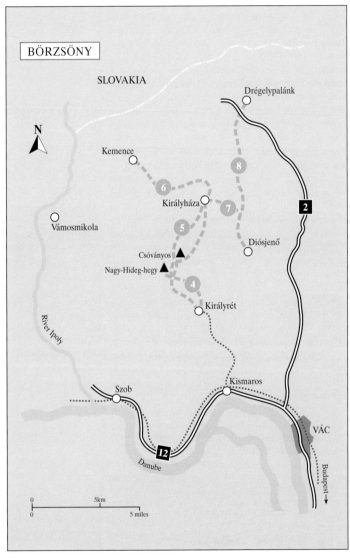

THE BÖRZSÖNY

Tucked neatly between the Danube Bend and the Slovakian border, the Börzsöny is easily overlooked, but the strenuous climb to its high ridges will dispel the popular notion that Hungary is a flat country. The range lies about 50km (30 miles) north of Budapest and is part of the Danube-Ipoly National Park. Its major summits are in the centre of the range: Csóványos is the highest at 938m (3076ft), Magosfa is 916m (3004ft), and Nagy-Hideg-hegy, the remains of a stratovolcano, 864m (2833ft). Much of the rock is

Nagy-Mána,
Börzsöny, Walk 5

andesite formed during the Miocene period when its central area was the core of Hungary's violent volcanic eruptions along a fault stretching as far as the Zemplén. The Börzsöny was part of the Visegrád mountain system until the end of the Pliocene Epoch when the Danube broke through to separate the two ranges and create the Dunakanyar (Danube Bend). The hills are cut in two by a deep valley (Kemencevölgy). Around the margins of the national park lies farmland. Raspberries are an important crop and the villages still have many old houses built in the style favoured by the Palóc people.

History

This was a region of migrations, and over the centuries Samartians, Quadii, Marcomanii, Celts, Huns, Goths and Longobards have passed through these mountains. It was at this frontier of the Roman Empire where Marcus Aurelius fought the Germanic tribes. Later came the nomadic Avars from the East who conquered the Slavs, but by the ninth century the region was part of the Moravian Empire. Many of the settlements along the Ipoly River were founded at the time of the early Magyars, but in 1241 the Mongol invasion forced the population to flee. Another period of instability and depopulation followed in the sixteenth century when the Ottomans invaded. In 1848 General Artúr Görgey led a daring winter expedition through the Börzsöny and went on to defeat the Habsburg army. Although Hungary was a German ally during much of World War II, an anti-Fascist partisan column named after Görgey operated in the hills. There is a monument commemorating their deeds in the village of Vámosmikola on the western side of the range.

Routes

Most casual day-trippers confine themselves to the steep walk up Csóványos and seem pleased with the view from its concrete observation tower, but the more adventurous walker can get most of the routes to him or herself. The walking is strenuous in places, but the effort is rewarded with plenty of panoramic views. Waymarked routes tend to radiate outwards like spokes in a wheel from the central area at Nagy-Hideg-hegy and some of the routes overlap and can be extended. Many of the forest tracks winding through the hills follow the routes of the old forest railways. The standard of waymarking is generally quite good, although the section of the National Blue Route between Csóványos and Nógrád is not recommended. If there is little time to explore the whole range the best route is Walk 5 to the Nagy-Mána ridge. The routes described are designed to begin and end at settlements with public transport links or accommodation. But the moderately fit walker should find it possible to arrive at a starting point in the morning, complete a walk, and still have time for refreshments before catching a train or bus back to Budapest on the same day.

Transport

Trains from Budapest Nyugati station or buses from Budapest Árpád híd arrive at Vác or Kismaros for local services on to the Börzsöny villages. A unique way into the centre of the hills is the little forest railway from Kismaros; it terminates at Királyrét, from where there are two or three walk-in points. There is also a forest train from the west valley walk-in point at Nagybörzsöny, but the walk up from Nagyirtás station is rather tedious. Timetables for both services are on the reverse of the Cartographia walking map. Getting back from the western slopes is by bus to Szob railway station. There are no buses along the road following the Kemence-völgy, and hitch-hiking is not recommended as there is little traffic.

Accommodation

As suggested in the transport section, the range is suitable for day walks using Budapest as a base, but a great way to get away from it all is to stay at one of the hostels near the summits. Nagy-Hideg-hegy *turistaház*, set just below the grass dome of the summit, has the most facilities, but Magas-Taxi *turistaház* is in a prettier setting; in autumn rutting stags challenge each other on the meadow in front of the hostel. In winter hostel beds are often full of skiers, but there is a good chance that there will be a few spaces in summer. As the hostels are at such a high elevation (Nagy-Hideg-hegy translates as Big Cold Mountain) even a midsummer evening is quite chilly so take a fleece for the evenings. The hotel in Királyrét is expensive and has monopolised accommodation in this popular starting-point for walks, but ask at the reception about vacancies in the cheaper *turistaszálló* opposite. Unfortunately the hostels at Királyháza in the Kemence-völgy require pre-booking. Most villages around the edge of the range have a selection of small hotels, guesthouses, private rooms and campsites with chalets for hire.

Points of interest in the Börzsöny

Diósjenő

The village has held on to some of its traditional peasant houses. One garden still has a traditional crane well.

Drégelypalánk

Drégely railway halt is a convenient place for the walk-in, but to visit the village alight at the next stop which is Drégelypalánk main station. The Baroque church owns a relic of Saint Elizabeth of Hungary and houses the Szondi family tomb.

Drégelyvár

The castle ruin perched on a volcanic cone is not visible on the approach, but after a hard climb the open aspect and view from its substantial ruins are reward enough. The castle saw service in 1556 when György Szondi defended it with only 146 Hungarians against 12,000 Ottoman troops led by the Pasha of Buda. It was a heroic struggle but the castle fell after four days.

Forest train

The little train journey from Kismaros to Királyrét is now a popular excursion for families, but the line was originally part of an extensive railway network constructed to carry timber down from the hills. Many of the old routes (marked *Régi vasút* on the map) are now walking paths. The introduction of heavy machinery, better forest roads and the reduction of clear-cutting in favour of selective harvesting have made the railways redundant, but the tourist trade has rescued this stretch of track and its rolling stock from the scrap yard.

Kemence

According to the historical records the first settlement here was founded 850 years ago. Today's buildings are not as old as that, but there are still fine examples of Palóc peasant houses. The large building passed on the left is the town hall and primary school and was built in 1750.

Királyrét

Its name, King's Meadow, implies that the area was a royal hunting ground. Apart from the forest workers gathering before work at the snack bar in the morning the village exists to cater for tourists and groups of children on field trips to study the flora and fauna. It is very busy on summer weekends as the good road and little forest train make for easy access. In winter skiing takes over.

Kőkorsó

Translated as stone jug, this outcrop and others like it in the area was formed at the beginning of the Quaternary period when volcanic activity resumed and the rocks of the Börzsöny were shattered. Csóványos and its immediate surroundings were raised and the basins sank while the movement created the large outcrops in the forests above Oltár-patak-völgy.

Magas-Tax hostel

The hostel is over 200 years old and it was originally a hunting lodge owned by an Austrian countess. It is named after the nearby volcanic hill of Magas Tax. The word *Magas* is Hungarian and means 'high', but the origins of *Tax* are obscure and it is not of Magyar origin.

WALK 4
Királyrét and Csóványos

Route:	Királyrét – Szállás-bérc – Csóványos – Nagy-Hideg-hegy/ Magas-Tax hostels – Királyrét
Distance:	22km (13.5 miles)
Map:	5 Börzsöny 1:40 000
Transport:	Get from Budapest to Kismaros and find the forest train terminus or bus stop for services to Királyrét. Cars or motorbikes are not permitted to drive all the way up to Nagy-Hideg-hegy but there is plenty of space to park a car at Királyrét. If not staying the night in one of the hostels and the last forest train has departed, there is an early evening bus from Királyrét back to Vác with connections to Budapest.
Refreshments:	Magas-Tax and Nagy-Hideg-hegy hostels offer meals and drinks to passing trade. On the return journey there is a hotel, restaurant and snack bar at Királyrét and a restaurant near Kismaros forest railway terminus.

This slightly strenuous circular route up and down the Börzsöny's highest summits affords some time to relax for refreshments at one of the hostels at the top. On tree-covered Csóványos climb the observation tower for a view or wait until Szabó-kövek ridge or the grassy pate of Nagy-Hideg-hegy.

At **Királyrét** follow the asphalt road leaving the village to the north and along a wall. Turn off at the first left on a blue-(square)-waymarked road. After a holiday house the little road becomes a hard-packed track passing along a fenced-off fishing lake. Eventually there is a barely visible pond up to the right. The trail splits; keep left to continue on the blue (square) route until another fork: take the right trail uphill through the woods to a stony track

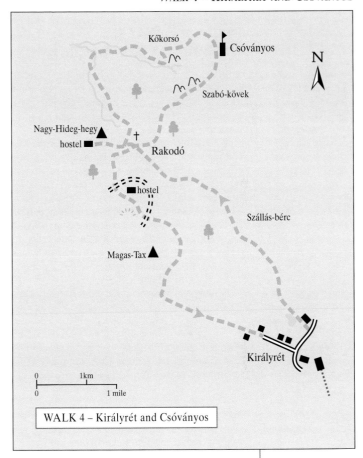

WALK 4 – Királyrét and Csóványos

and turn left. From here the long straight track takes about an hour to ascend the spur of Szállás-bérc. Note that half-way up the waymarks change to blue (O). At the top there is a fork; veer left to join the rutted forest track continuing on the blue (O) waymarks. The track contours and undulates around the forest for about half an hour until it

Diversion

The walk will pass Nagy-Hideg-hegy and Magas-Tax hostels on the return leg but it is a good idea to take the opportunity to book into one of the hostels and dump any excess weight before continuing. If so, do not go up to the saddle ahead but turn left along the blue-(+)-waymarked track. The track contours the forested slopes for about a quarter of an hour until it joins the red-waymarked route. At the good forest track turn right and then leave it at the first path left for Magas-Tax hostel. For Nagy-Hideg-hegy turn right at the red-waymarked track to follow the spur up to the summit.

comes to a crossroads of trails and a blue (+) track veering left. ◀

If not diverting to the hostels ignore the blue (+) track and continue uphill to the Rakodó saddle and its confusion of waymarked trails. On the left an eroded ski-run comes down the spur and over to the right a large wooden cross devoted to Saint Stephen is visible. To continue from Rakodó keep straight ahead on the narrow blue-(O)-waymarked path descending the other side of the saddle. Cross straight over the first good forest track and continue downhill on the little path. Turn left on the blue-(+)-waymarked path which drops rather steeply down a forested valley. After about half an hour the path bottoms out at a clearing and passes a hunting hide before coming to a junction of trails. Turn right for the blue (triangle) path and cross the stream. On the other side the path veers left and approaches a meadow with another hunting hide but before that turn right for the blue (triangle) trail going up into the woods.

As the path rises sharply uphill through the forest it veers slightly right, from where the long hunting meadow is visible down on the left. The path eventually enters the Oltár-patak-völgy. When the trail crosses the stream to join another path turn right on the blue (triangle) waymarks. The route traverses up the other side of the valley crossing the stream a couple of times. Soon, the valley closes in and has outcrops looming high up the slope. Where the valley bifurcates turn left across the stream to a boulder with a painted waymark. The blue (triangle) trail now zigzags up the steep hill to **Kőkorsó** outcrop.

After the outcrop the trail continues up a wooded spur eventually veering left to more outcrops offering rather limited views to the west, but press on to the top where the path joins another trail. Turn right to follow the red- and green-waymarked route. The trail is quite level at first but begins to ascend a steep spur to the summit of Csóványos. Swing around to the right of the observation tower with its fluttering Hungarian flag and after the peace monument veer right for the red and blue waymarks heading down another steep spur.

From here the walk descends through forest and passes the rock outcrops of Szabó-kövek and along open sections of ridge until the familiar Rakodó saddle is reached. Continue past the wooden cross following the red- and blue-waymarked track contouring the

Peace Walk Monument, Csóványos

left of the hill. Take the next red/blue route turning right to climb a steep forested slope to Nagy-Hideg-hegy. Once out of the woods the hostel is to the left. For Magas-Tax hostel start at the front door of Nagy-Hideg-hegy hostel and descend the grassy slope and pick up the red and red (square) trail. The trail follows electricity pylons for a while but soon re-enters the forest and winds down a spur to a blue (+) track. Continue to the good forest road, turn right along it for a few metres and leave at the first left for Magas-Tax hostel.

Starting at Magas-Tax hostel return to Királyrét by heading straight across the meadow. Veer left and join the good forest track. Follow it left for a few paces before turning right on a red-waymarked track contouring the forested hill called Magas-Tax. On the other side it joins a long broad stony firebreak with a line of pylons along its length. Turn left and follow it all the way to the bottom. At a barrier the track becomes a road and passes orchards, raspberry gardens, a forest lodge and an old sawmill. Where it joins a good road turn left for the last 200m or so into Királyrét.

WALK 5
Nagy-Mána Ridge

This is probably the Börzsöny's most spectacular route and is particularly suitable for walkers staying at one of the hostels. Allow some time to dally on the Nagy-Mána ridge for lunch and to take plenty of photographs of the best panorama in the range. In summer look out for sand lizards basking on the sun-baked rocks and fire salamanders in the cooler valley floors. The return walk is along the deserted Rózsa-völgy followed by a long climb up to the earth ramparts of Pogányvár and on to Csóványos. In summer this is a dry walk and the path is clear of vegetation, but there are steep descents with loose stones. It is

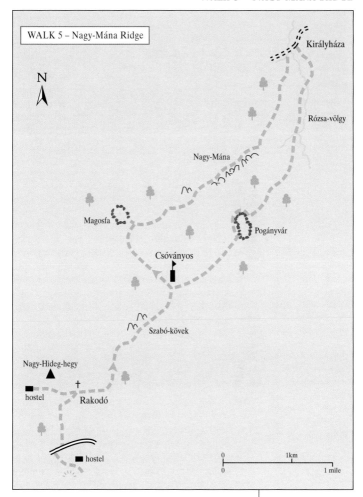

clear from Cartographia's map that there are many possible walks based on this route but not all of them work. See Walks 6 and 7 for variations.

Route:	Nagy-Hideg-hegy/Magas-Tax hostels – Csóványos – Nagy-Mána – Pogányvár – Csóványos – Szabó-kövek – Nagy-Hideg-hegy/Magas-Tax hostels
Distance:	15km (9.5 miles)
Map:	5 Börzsöny 1:40 000
Transport:	A circular route suitable for walkers staying at Nagy-Hideg-hegy or Magas-Tax hostel. If driving, start at a different point in the loop by parking at Királyháza in Kemence-völgy and walk the short distance to the entrance of Rózsa-völgy and pick up the walk up to Pogányvár.
Refreshments:	Take a packed lunch and plenty of water. After the descent from Nagy-Mána do not detour to Királyháza expecting to find refreshments.

From Nagy-Hideg-hegy hostel

Take the red and blue track contouring the grassy summit of Nagy-Hideg-hegy and turn right for the steep path down through the woods. When the path joins a track, turn left for the trail junction at Rakodó.

From Magas-Tax hostel

Face the meadow in front of the building and turn sharp right and pass the WC. Pick up the trail going through the trees. At the forest road turn right, and after a short stretch turn left for the red-waymarked track. Pick up the blue (+) track and follow it as it contours the woods. After about a quarter of an hour it rises to the trail junction on the Rakodó saddle.

Continuing from the Rakodó saddle follow the red- and blue-waymarked route which passes the wooden cross dedicated to Saint Stephen. From here the trail begins to climb one of Csóványos's wooded spurs, but the tree cover gives way here and there to grassy ridges, most notably at Szabó-kövek. After one last steep section the path tops out on Csóványos. Veer left to pass the peace monument and swing around the other side of the concrete observation tower. On the other side bear left and descend the little path with red, green and blue (triangle) waymarks. The trail follows the steep drop of the forested spur and, after levelling off for a while, passes the turn-off for the blue (triangle) route. But continue on the red and green waymarks as the trail rises slightly to a fork. The path on the left is for the Iron Age fort ruins on the summit of Magosfa but it is not worth the diversion. Turn right to follow the red waymarks descending another steep and wooded spur. At the level ground a red (square) trail leaves left but ignore it and continue straight ahead. The walking is pleasant here and the red waymarks take the trail along a broad grassy ridge with scattered trees, but do not miss the red waymarks indicating where the route drops steeply right. After descending through thick woodland the ground levels, but the narrow track soon begins to rise again to the ridge leading up to Nagy-Mána. From here the trees thin out on the narrowing ridge to give views of the deep valley of Rózsa-völgy and the forested dome of Pogányvár.

Looking up Rózsa-völgy

81

The highest point of Nagy-Mána is the large out-crop jutting out over the valley, after which the route continues along a broad grassy ridge. At the end of the spur turn left for the path dropping sharply down in among the trees. It is a long descent on the rocky path winding down through the forest. At the valley bottom cross the stream, turn right along a track, and then cross another stream. Follow the track a short while and turn right on the red (triangle) waymarks into the long valley of Rózsa-völgy. Floods have destroyed sections of the old forest railway embankment along which the original route passed, but cross the stream to pick up the fresher waymarks marking the good track up on the right bank.

The trail rises above the stream and after about a quarter of an hour the valley bifurcates. The route is badly waymarked here but drop down left and cross the stream to find the continuation of the red (triangle) path which begins to climb the steep spur between the two burns. It is a hard slog from here until the Iron Age ramparts of Pogányvár where the slope becomes gentler. The path swings around the remains of the rampart until an old fence. On the other side follow the steep trail down to a meadow. Continue up the next spur, through a conifer plantation to join a forest track. The red (triangle) waymarks guide the remaining route up to the familiar summit of Csóványos. Retrace steps back to the hostels by following the red and blue waymarks down to the Rakodó saddle.

WALK 6
Nagy-Hideg-hegy to Kemence

This is a variation on Walk 5 and is suitable for linking other parts of the range via the high Nagy-Mána route. Instead of returning to the hostels it finishes at the village of Kemence on the north-west side of the Börzsöny. The walk is suitable if starting from the Nagy-Hideg-hegy or Magas-Tax hostels, but unless

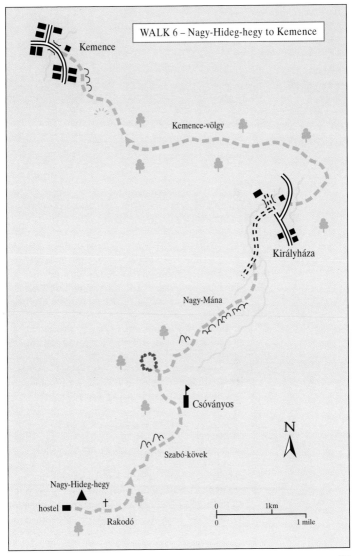

WALK 6 – Nagy-Hideg-hegy to Kemence

Kemence

Kemence-völgy

Királyháza

Nagy-Mána

Csóványos

N

Szabó-kövek

Nagy-Hideg-hegy

hostel

Rakodó

0		1km
0		1 mile

Route:	Nagy-Hideg-hegy hostel – Csóványos – Nagy-Mána – Királyháza – Kemence
Distance:	19km (11.5 miles)
Map:	5 Börzsöny 1:40 000
Transport:	If planning to get back to Budapest the same day there are evening buses from Kemence (although it may be necessary to change buses at Vámosmikola) to Szob railway station with train connections.
Refreshments:	None until Kemence where there are shops, bars and a restaurant.

booked accommodation awaits at Kemence the whole walk from Királyrét (see Walk 4) is only recommended for the fleet of foot.

Follow the route instructions in Walk 5 but after the descent from Nagy-Mána ridge do not go up Rózsa-völgy but continue on the red-waymarked track for the hunting lodge road. Turn right and join the asphalt road and then turn left. After a group of buildings on the left pick up a little path on the right dropping down a bank to cross a stream on stepping-stones. On the other side gain the rough track which rises steeply through the forest.

At the top of the broad and forested ridge turn left to follow the yellow-waymarked track along the long shoulder. After about an hour and a half there is a meadow with a hunting tower, after which the track swings right and descends to another meadow with a national park sign. From here walk for about a hundred metres to a crossroads of old and overgrown tracks. Take the vague grassy track left. It passes an old fence to descend through woodland and past some old wine cellars set into the bank on the right. At the bottom the track leaves the woods and enters the village of **Kemence**. Turn right, then left over the bridge, then right past the school building to the bus stop and most of the village facilities.

WALK 7
Királyháza to Diósjenő

Route:	Királyháza – Bugyihó – Csánki-kert – Kámor – Csepegő-kő – Diósjenő
Distance:	22km (13.5 miles)
Map:	5 Börzsöny 1:40 000
Transport:	Start at the hostels around Nagy-Hideg-hegy. At the end of the walk local trains from Diósjenő terminate at Vác, from where there are connections to Budapest.
Refreshments:	None until Diósjenő. There is a bar at the railway station.

This is another variation on Walk 5 and is best started after an overnight stay at one of the hostels around Nagy-Hideg-hegy. If depending on public transport to get back to Budapest the same day set a cracking pace. The route takes in the wonderful Nagy-Mána ridge. Waymarking is poor on the approach to the hill called Kámor and the route is overgrown. On the descent to the village of Diósjenő the view from Csepegő-kő, taking in the lowlands of Nógrád, is spectacular.

Follow the route instructions in Walk 5 but after the descent from Nagy-Mána ridge do not go up Rózsa-völgy but continue on the red-waymarked track for the hunting lodge road. Turn right and join the asphalt road and then turn left. After a group of buildings on the left pick up a little path on the right dropping down a bank to cross a stream on stepping-stones. On the other side gain the rough track which rises steeply through the forest.

At the top of the broad and forested ridge turn right to follow the yellow-waymarked route to Bugyihó. The track veers around the left of the summit, but it is possible to pick a way up through the woods to the crag for a good view across the

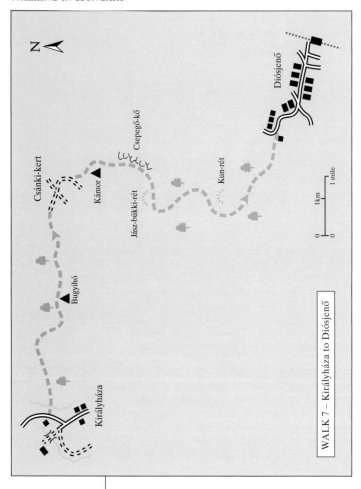

WALK 7 – Királyháza to Diósjenő

Börzsöny. From here the waymarking is erratic but keep following the track until it traverses downhill to the right to the crossroads at Csánki-kert.

Turn left to follow a rutted track. The trees have been felled and waymarks are missing, but this is the yellow route. The track descends, but as it levels and begins to swing right look in the long grass and bushes on the left for a footpath. There are still no waymarks and the path is overgrown, but head across the area of scattered bushes towards the woods. Once in among the trees pick up the few faded yellow waymarks guiding the route uphill. The going levels as the spur becomes broader but bear left to maintain height and then veer right for the summit of Kámor. Cross over the hilltop to the other side, where an overgrown footpath descends to the crags of Csepegő-kő.

After admiring the view turn away from the crag to pick up the continuation of the narrow trail. It descends at a safe distance from the edge. At the bottom the path levels, crosses a track and enters woodland. To the right is the meadow of Jász-bükki-rét with a hunting tower. Cross a small section of woodland over a finger of the meadow and then turn right to follow the forest edge. Turn left at the next grassy track; it swings around the wooded spur of Jász-bükk descending the other side to another meadow called Kun-rét. Follow the track across and around the meadow. It winds left turning into woodland down to a cleared area usually used as a car park and turning point for forestry lorries. Cut straight across to the edge of a steep slope and pick up the steep narrow path through the woods. The path descends the steep slope to join a broader forest track and eventually joins an old stony forest road. After leaving the woods the national park office and a camping chalet complex are passed just before **Diósjenő**. Follow the street called Petőfi út and take the long and wide avenue leading to the railway station.

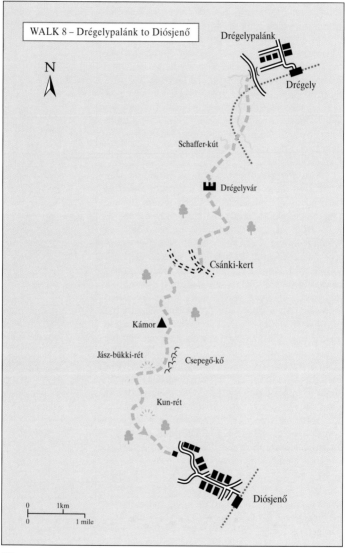

WALK 8 – Drégelypalánk to Diósjenő

N

Drégelypalánk

Drégely

Schaffer-kút

Drégelyvár

Csánki-kert

Kámor

Jász-bükki-rét

Csepegő-kő

Kun-rét

Diósjenő

0   1km

0   1 mile

WALK 8
Drégelypalánk to Diósjenő

Route:	Drégely railway halt – Drégelyvár – Kámor – Csepegő-kő – Diósjenő railway station
Distance:	17.5km (11 miles)
Map:	5 Börzsöny 1:40 000
Transport:	From Vác there are local trains to Drégely halt. If depending on public transport to get back to Budapest the same night, do not leave the descent into Diósjenő too late as trains and buses back to Vác are few and far between.
Refreshments:	None until Diósjenő. There is a bar at the railway station.

Most of the route is through forest, but the uphill bits are rewarded with good views. A half-day walk at speed, but it is best taken at a leisurely pace, stopping at the crags of Csepegő-kő for lunch with panorama. Waymarking is poor on the approach to Kámor where the route is overgrown. In order to avoid repetition of text, the route description from the crossroads at Csánki-kert is in Walk 7.

Start at Drégely railway halt at the southern end of **Drégelypalánk**. Cross the railway and take the road down over a little bridge. Turn left, picking up the red-waymarked asphalt road which becomes a sandy track and passes under a road bridge for Highway 2. The track crosses the railway a couple of times before coming to a meadow. Head straight between the picnic table and the Schaffer-kút spring for the red-waymarked trail winding uphill. It soon joins a wider track and then crosses another, but let the red waymarks guide the route until the turning on the red (L) waymarks and the last five minutes' climb to **Drégelyvár** fortress ruin.

Walk the length of the ruins and down the other side to rejoin the red (L) route. There is a junction of tracks but continue straight ahead on the blue waymarks. The track descends across a cleared area back into woodland. After the picnic site take the track right, continuing on the blue waymarks. Follow the track up the wooded spur and down the other side passing a felled area. The main track swings right to descend, but continue straight ahead on an overgrown path which traverses gently downhill to a forest road. Cross over the road and veer right heading for a large cleared area. Keep to the right and straight ahead to find a blue-(square)-waymarked track rising through the woods to an asphalt road. Turn right and follow the road as it swings left. The road passes a turn-off for a quarry but continue until the blue (square) waymarks for a trail climbing the left bank. After traversing through the forest, the trail joins a track; follow it left to exit the forest at a saddle and junction of tracks. Continue downhill to a crossroads of rutted tracks marked Csánki-kert on the map.

For the remaining route refer to the route instructions from Csánki-kert in Walk 7.

THE BÜKK

The word *bükk* is of non-Magyar origin and refers to the beech trees for which this range is famous, although hornbeam and oak are also in abundance, with juniper and karst meadow a regular feature on the highest elevations. The gentle climb up through forest to the 900m (2900ft) summits is deceptive, and it is only once its great limestone outcrops are reached that the walker can get a feel for the elevation. Situated 130km (80 miles) north-east of Budapest between the cities of Eger and Miskolc, the Bükk is reputed to be the oldest range in Hungary.

Őr-kő, Bükk-fennsík, Bükk, Walk 9

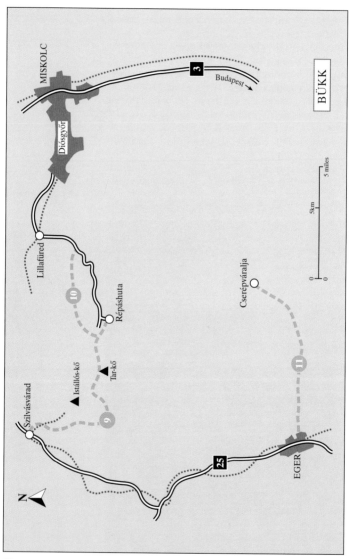

Formed 300 million years ago from tropical seabed sediment, it was later raised to become the limestone block of the high plateau, or Bükk-fennsík. Many valleys dissect the plateau, notably the north–south Hórvölgy and east–west Garadna-völgy. Layers of rhyolite caused by the volcanic eruptions of the Miocene Epoch have left behind the soft tufa characteristic of the southern slope of the range, the Bükkalja. Here in the lower hills there is farmland, and the volcanic soil supports viticulture. The terraced vineyards around Eger produce the famous full-bodied red wine called Egri Bikavér (Bull's Blood).

History

'Kerget a tatár?' (Are the Tartars chasing you?) is the Hungarian equivalent of the English saying 'Where's the fire?' After the defeat of the Hungarian army at Muhi, King Béla IV galloped across the Bükk with the army of Genghis Khan's grandson close on his heels. The Bükk continued to bear the brunt of history when Hussites occupied the hilltop forts and plundered the surrounding villages. King Matthias drove the Hussites out in 1472, but in the sixteenth century the region fell under the Ottoman sword and many settlements were abandoned.

Today the high trails are peaceful and the valley settlements popular with tourists, but the Bükk has long been associated with industry dating back to the Iron Age and the Celts. In the Middle Ages, lime extracted from the karst woodlands was used in the construction of the castle of Eger. During the eighteenth century settlers came to the remote forest valleys to work in the glass foundries, quarry for slate and burn charcoal. Many abandoned lime-kilns (a few operated until the early 1980s) are scattered around the hills. From the late eighteenth century Diósgyőr to the east of the range became the second most important producer of iron in the Habsburg Empire. Charcoal burners still operate in parts of the forest, and today the descendants of the eighteenth-century settlers, Slovaks, Germans, Moravians, Poles and Serbs, continue to live in and around these hills. To get a feel for the Bükk's industrial history visit the open-air forest museum in the valley of Szalajka-völgy south of Szilvásvárad.

A unique feature of the southern part of the Bükk is the large number of caves dug into the soft rhyolite. Often set deep in the forest they served as stables or sheep barns or perhaps shelters for herders and beekeepers. There are also caves behind village houses; these are former dwellings and have provided refuge from invading armies for centuries – recently during World War II. Many families continued to live in the caves up until the 1970s, but most have been converted into wine cellars or summer kitchens.

Beehive Stones

Hungary's mysterious beehive stones (*kaptárkő*), some as high as 13m (40ft), stand deep in the forests of the Bükkalja. These eroded rhyolite cones were formed by volcanic and thermal activity during the Miocene Epoch. There are over 100 beehive stones in Hungary and 72 of them are in the Bükk, and it is thought that there are more examples to be discovered. An unusual feature is the rectangular compartments cut into the soft stone. They are quite unique to Hungary although there are similar examples in Bulgaria, Turkey and Iran, prompting speculation about their origin. Legends and theories about the purpose of the stones abound: Celtic sacrifice altars; the gravestones of Hun warriors; resting places for the ashes of Magyar chieftains killed in the pagan uprisings; or Hussite worship sites. The theory most favoured by historians is that bees were kept in the compartments, but whether the forest apiarists were Ottomans or Hussites is not known. A few beehive stones can be reached after a short walk from a conveniently parked car, but many require a compass and involve a good deal of bashing through brambles. The stones are marked on Cartographia's maps using the same black triangular symbols denoting rock outcrops, but are distinguished from other rhyolite obtrusions by the word *kaptárkő* or *kaptárkövek*. They make excellent viewpoints and places to stop for refreshments, but please try not to add to the erosion.

Routes

The walks in the guide concentrate on the central high plateau of the Bükk-fennsík and the lower southern hills of the Bükkalja. The routes described below represent only a small selection of the potential walks in such a large range, but if exploring other parts of the Bükk avoid the stony track through the long valley of Hór-völgy which links Bogács in the south to Lillafüred in the north. Not only is it boring, but locals and tourists drive their cars along the unsurfaced forest track at speed, kicking up loose stones and dust. Istállós-kő at 959m (3145ft) is the Bükk's highest hill, but the long and exhausting climb from Szilvásvárad is a disappointment as trees obscure the view from the summit. The two Bükk-fennsík walks in the guide offer opportunities for panoramic views from the limestone outcrops of the southern escarpment. Many waymarked routes in the Bükkalja have fallen into disuse, but the walk described below provides an interesting excursion taking in village life and a few beehive stones.

Transport

There are regular trains from Budapest Keleti to Miskolc and Eger. Change for Szilvásvárad. From the bus station at Budapest Népstadion there are good services for Eger but fewer direct buses to Miskolc and Szilvásvárad. A jolly way to get to the tourist resort of Lillafüred is on the Lillafüred Forest Railway (LÁEV) from Miskolc. Alternatively there are buses from Diósgyőr. Regular buses ply between Eger and Mezőkövesd linking the Bükkalja villages.

Accommodation

The popular holiday resort of Szilvásvárad is well placed for access to the routes and has plenty of accommodation including a campsite, but expect higher than average prices. There is a useful street map of the town on the reverse of Cartographia's map 33 showing the important places and a few hotels. Although there are no villages on the long route across the Bükk-fennsík, the walker happy to carry a sleeping bag, food and water will find a cave refuge at Cserepes-kő marked *Barlangszállás* on map 33 (map reference: 189221). Facilities are basic but there are bed platforms and a stove, although the nearest spring is quite far. Leave the cave and the surrounding area clean and tidy and take your rubbish with you. Private rooms are available in Répáshuta and there is a campsite, although the latter is open for a very short summer period.

Points of interest in the Bükk

Bogács

The village has long attracted visitors to its thermal baths but since the 1990s the village has experienced rapid development to cater for the increase in tourists. The men sitting outside the cellars are hoping to entice travellers in to sample their wine. The villagers belong to the Matyó people found throughout the county and they have a distinctive folk costume.

Cserépváralja

Its name, Foot of the Tiled Castle, remembers the fort that once stood on the hill above the village. During the sixteenth century there was a small Ottoman garrison here, but its eventual destruction probably took place during the 1703–11 War of Independence against Austria. Access to the ruins is via the youth camp when the gates are not locked. According to the locals the site is hardly worth a visit as the rubble was recycled to build the village houses and the little chapel on the hill (now the youth camp canteen). The museum on Gárdonyi utca 5 has a typical cave-dwelling.

Cserepes-kő barlangszállás
In 1950 Dr Sándor Kertay, József Bárdos and István Franczia converted this old cave into a walker's refuge.

Eger
Picturesque and historic Eger has cobbled streets, pleasant squares, eighteenth-century houses, a basilica and a castle, so it is worth staying a couple of days. One of Hungary's rare military successes took place here in 1552 when the castle was successfully held against a numerically and technically superior Ottoman army. The famous Egri Bikavér (Bull's Blood) made locally gets its name from the tradition that the castle defenders drank wine mixed with bull's blood in the belief that it would increase their strength.

Erdei Múzeum
This outdoor exhibition of forest industry through the ages includes reconstructed foresters' huts, lime and glass kilns, and smelting equipment. The iron sign with the date 1834 was made locally and its inscription reads: 'No fishing, you ruffian!'

Erdészeti Múzeum
This interesting museum of the social and natural history of the Bükk opens as early as 8.30am.

Fátyol-vízesés
Tourist brochures make a great fuss about this rather disappointing series of small waterfalls, emphasising the fact that surface streams are rare in the karstic hills. The water here is particularly suitable for breeding trout, introduced in the nineteenth century. This is one of the few places in Hungary frequented by dippers, a small land bird adapted to swim underwater to catch insects.

Forest workers' monument
There is a beautiful setting for this tasteful memorial dedicated to the many forest workers who have died in accidents.

Jubileumi körtúra
The yellow-waymarked Jubilee Way was set up in 1992 to celebrate the hundredth anniversary of the first organised walks in the Bükk.

Lillafüred

Count András Bethlen, Hungary's Minister for Agriculture, created this resort in 1891 and named it after his wife, Lilla. There are caves to visit and a lake with little boats for hire if staying for a few days.

Mária-bánya

This old mine was a source of iron ore in the eighteenth century.

Nagy-mező

The Nagy-mező is a nature reserve of sink-holes, karst grassland and juniper. The rather obtrusive signs leave the walker in no doubt that camping, lighting fires, picnics, leaving the waymarked route and picking flowers are forbidden. Unfortunately the asphalt road cutting an unsightly gash through this interesting landscape makes a mockery of these admonitions. Until recently the good road enabled day-trippers to drive up here but today the meadow is out of bounds to vehicles. The average elevation of 800m (2600ft) combined with temperature inversion in sink-holes can cause the temperature to drop below freezing on a summer night, providing a micro-climate suitable for rare plants normally found in the Carpathians.

Répáshuta

On the rough road leaving south there is a little waymarked track for the Balla cave. Excavations in the cave have uncovered the bones of a bear, hyena and buffalo; stone tools; and the skull of a child. Germans and Slovaks settled the area in the eighteenth century to work in the glass foundries (*üveghuta*) making bottles for the Tokaj vineyards. The first foundry, at Gyertyán-völgy, a valley 2km (about a mile) to the east, operated until 1897. Traces of the original settlement survive. Slavic speech has influenced the local Hungarian dialect. The museum on Szabadság utca 5 describes village life between the two world wars.

Soldiers' graves

Soldiers' graves (*katonasírok*) dotted around the hills are a reminder that thousands of Russian, German and Hungarian soldiers died in the Bükk in World War II. Soon after a battle front had passed through, local forestry workers and walkers would come to the hills to bury the dead. Many bodies ended up in a mass grave or were eventually reburied in local cemeteries, but there are probably hundreds still to be found. On All Saints' Day some associations organise walks to place flowers on the graves and light candles in memory of the fallen. There is now a scheme for German families who want to retrieve the bodies of their relatives. The inscription on one of the graves in Horotna-völgy says:

> *Do not pick the flower in the meadow*
> *But look upon it,*
> *Caress it.*
> *And sprinkle it with tears of blood.*

Soviet Army Monument

The local council erected this monument at this site which saw a bloody battle between Ukrainian and German troops in World War II. The inscription on this monument reads:

> *They came from where the Don flows.*
> *Give them Hungarian soil,*
> *For a soft resting place.*

There is also a plaque down in Szomolya on Bercsényi út 8 dedicated to a Soviet radio operator called Klara who was executed by German soldiers.

Szalajka Valley Forest Train (SÁEV)

This little train was once part of the Bükk railway on which engines shunted all the way up to Bánkút. As recently as 1966 the little steam railway transported limestone from the mine below Istállós-kő to Szilvásvárad. Some of the walking trails pass along the route of the old railway – marked *Régi vasút* on the map.

Szalajka-völgy

When it was a centre of iron smelting this valley was called Vasgyár-völgy (Iron Factory Valley). Today's name comes from a Slovak word for ash-grease, a component used in glass-making. Trout breeding pools can be seen along the road after the first fishing pond.

Szikla-forrás

The Bükk karst provides drinking water for about half a million people and, depending on the year's rainfall, this spring produces up to 10,000 litres of water a minute.

Szilvásvárad

Szilvásvárad is a charmless holiday resort but is well placed for walking. The town is famous for its Lippizaner stud farm and unusual horse graves. Every August there is an international horse show and festival.

Szomolya

For some reason its name comes from the Slovak word *smola* (wax or tar) but it is more famous for its delicious black cherries. After the church, turn left for the cave houses where even the better-off smallholders once lived. One of the caves has been converted into a rather sterile museum, but for a more authentic experience of cave life walk up to the right to view one that is still occupied.

Szomolya Beehive Stones

Of the three groups of beehive stones, Szomolya is the most visible because the surrounding trees have been felled. It has a charming legend set during the Ottoman occupation. A group of Hungarian soldiers were carrying the Diósgyőr garrison payroll when the Turks gave chase. To outwit their pursuers the soldiers carved the holes in the stones to make them look like the windows of a fort. On seeing this rather impressive stronghold the Turks fled.

WALK 9
The High Bükk:
Szilvásvárad to Répáshuta

Route:	Szilvásvárad – Szalajka-völgy – Őr-kő – Cserepes-kő – Tar-kő – Három-kő – Répáshuta
Distance:	22.5km (14 miles)
Map:	33 Bükk-fennsík 1:40 000
Transport:	Cut out the initial walk-in by catching the Szalajka Valley Forest Train (SÁEV) (runs April to November) from Szilvásvárad (Szalajkavölgy-Lovaspálya station on Egri út). The timetable is on the reverse of the map. At the end of the walk there are buses from Répáshuta to Miskolc. At Miskolc bus station find the underpass/subway to get to the busy main street and trams for Miskolc-Tiszai railway station for Budapest trains.
Refreshments:	Pack food and plenty of water and relax on one of the limestone outcrops. Répáshuta has two bars and a restaurant offering game dishes.

The walk soon leaves the snack bars and gift shops of Szilvásvárad behind to climb the forested slopes of the Bükk-fennsík. Joining the National Blue Route the walk passes limestone outcrops with excellent views and there is plenty of interest: war graves, abandoned lime-kilns and old beech forest. Good waymarking guides the walker along pleasant winding tracks, although there is loose rock on some descents. There are short stretches of asphalt at either end of the walk but the road is not busy. Unless planning to stay at the Cserepes-kő cave refuge, start as early as possible to complete this walk in a day and have enough time for refreshments at Répáshuta.

Leave **Szilvásvárad** from its south-east corner along Szalajka út passing a row of bars and gift shops. The

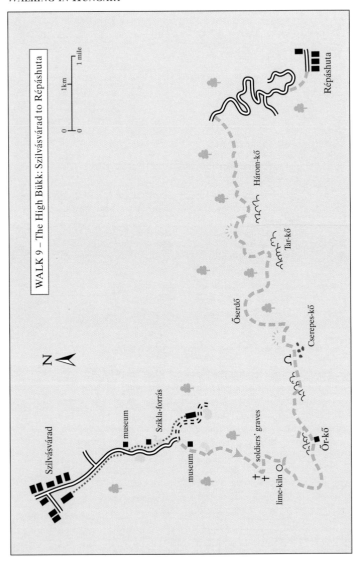

WALK 9 – The High Bükk: Szilvásvárad to Répáshuta

N

Szilvásvárad

museum

Szikla-forrás

museum

soldiers' graves

lime-kiln

Őr-kő

Cserepes-kő

Őserdő

Tar-kő

Három-kő

Répáshuta

0   1km

0   1 mile

road leaves the village to follow **Szalajka-völgy** passing the little game park (*Vadaspark*), **Erdészeti Múzeum**, fish pond, and trout-breeding pools. After passing the **Szikla-forrás** gushing out of the rocks leave the asphalt road on a track down to the right and cross the wooden bridge and pick up the yellow-and green-waymarked route to the open air **Erdei Múzeum**. ▶

Go through the open ground and pass the exhibits of the Erdei Múzeum to pick up the footpath at the other end. After the last information board take a narrow path which climbs the bank on the right. The path turns right to skirt around a pond and then left to join a yellow-waymarked path. From here the straight, narrow path is a little overgrown but bear with it until it exits at a forest track. Cross straight over the track and follow the trail up the valley, passing the entrance for **Mária-bánya**. As the path approaches the top it veers right to climb a bank. At the broad saddle with a junction of forest tracks bear left past the **soldiers' graves** and follow the wide track

Őr-kő, Bükk-fennsík

Alternative Route
If taking the little train from Szilvásvárad, get off at Halastó railway halt to visit the Erdészeti Múzeum or stay on until the Fátyol-vízesés terminus and backtrack downstream, passing the waterfall and eventually turning left for the yellow-and green-waymarked route to the Erdei Múzeum.

Diversion

From the meadow
take the little
footpath left. Head
through a gap in the
rocks with a blue
(triangle) waymark
and veer left up the
hill to gain the Őr-kő
outcrop. It is a five-
minute walk to the
top. There is a good
view across the hills
to Eger. Return to
the meadow and
crossroads the
same way.

ahead. After a few paces peel off right, joining the narrower track with blue, red and yellow waymarks.

Continue uphill as the track winds up through karst woodland passing the remains of an old lime-kiln. At a fork the red route peels off but continue on the blue- and yellow-waymarked track, the **Jubileumi körtúra**. From here the blue waymarks take the route around Ördög-hegy (Devil's Hill) through conifer woods and across a meadow. The path passes below the rocks of Őr-kő and after the hunting lodge rises to a small meadow and cross-roads of faint grassy tracks. ◀

Starting at the meadow continue in the original direction to a fork. Ignore the confusing set of blue (+) and red waymarks but take the right track, eventually picking up the blue waymarks. The path undulates through the woods for a while but do not follow it down to another meadow; take the narrower footpath climbing sharply right. Let the blue waymarks guide the route along a raised rocky section, almost a ridge. The meandering path begins a steep descent through the Pes-kő-kapu boulders. There is a fine view where the boulders break out from the trees but there is better ahead so continue downhill. At a saddle cross over the broad track and veer left for the blue-waymarked path traversing down the right side of a valley. The path eventually swings left to join the green (square) route on the left slope. The joint waymarks now traverse the other side of the valley below Cserepes-kő spur. ◀

Diversion

The path up to the
cave refuge called
**Cserepes-kő
barlangszállás** is a
short detour on the
green (square)
waymarks.

The blue-waymarked path continues over and around the other side of Cserepes-kő, after which the trail breaks up and disappears as it winds through the karst woodland. Maintain height and keep an eye on the blue waymarks. The rocky section is left behind eventually and the going is easier as the path rises and traverses to the right out onto the steep rocky meadow marked on the map as *Szép kilátás!* Admire the view before re-entering the forest, where the path gently descends to a spur switching back to contour the other side. After a while the track veers left and merges with the green route. Continue on the Blue Route up and around the old beech woods at **Őserdő** and down the other side to where the two waymarks part company. Keep left to stay on the blue-way-marked track, and it begins to climb steeply up to the second outcrop, Tar-kő. To gain the crags and a stunning view turn right on a little path with blue (square) waymarks for the last few metres to the summit.

From Tar-kő find the blue waymarks by following the edge of the rocks and veering left past a signpost, survey pillar and National Blue Route stamping point back into the forest. The path now descends to follow a fence for a while before becoming a broader track undulating through the woods and crossing a meadow. At the junction of trails turn right on the green-(triangle)-waymarked path which crosses a little meadow before ascending gently through hazel scrub to the broad meadow and crags of Három-kő. This is the last and probably the best panorama of the walk and a commanding position from which to see falcons and eagles. It is worth dallying here for a while.

To finish the walk bear left away from the edge of Három-kő and head for the trees to pick up a grassy track skirting the woods. Green (triangle) waymarks indicate the route back into the forest. The route descends to a level area at a fork; take the right track passing a game feeder. Here the path narrows and waymarks are absent, but stay on the well-trodden path ignoring any left turnings. Descend the other side of the hill and continue across a hollow with a scattering of trees. Continue straight ahead on a little path through scrub, and after a long stretch of contouring through woodland a broader track is joined. Turn right and after a short walk an asphalt road appears. Turn right again to follow the road for a couple of minutes until the next right, a red-waymarked grassy track flanking a fence. The track descends to a corner of the fence; keep

straight ahead. At the next junction turn left to follow the green (square) waymarks. Let the waymarks
guide the convoluted trail downhill until the forest
road joins the main road at a little house and information board. Turn left to follow the road for about
ten minutes before taking the second turning right
for a footpath descending a little valley into
Répáshuta.

WALK 10
The High Bükk:
Lillafüred to Répáshuta

Route:	Lillafüred – Lusta-völgy – Nagy-mező – Három-kő – Répáshuta
Distance:	24km (15 miles)
Map:	33 Bükk-fennsík 1:40 000
Transport:	To get to Lillafüred catch the forest train from Miskolc LÁEV or a bus from Diósgyőr bus station.
Refreshments:	Eat a packed lunch on Három-kő limestone outcrop and watch the swooping falcons or tumbling ravens. There is a good restaurant in Répáshuta.

An alternative route across the Bükk-fennsík, this
time from east to west. Good waymarking guides
the walker along a section of the Bükki kék (Bükk
Blue Route). The walking passes through the amaz-
ing karst meadows of Nagy-mező and offers a
panoramic view from Három-kő limestone outcrop.
Tracks and paths are good but the walk-in and walk-
off involve some road walking, although traffic is
light. The asphalt road crossing parts of the Bükk-
fennsík is intrusive but facilitates a good pace. King
Béla IV on his retreat from the Battle of Muhi in
1241 would have been glad of it.

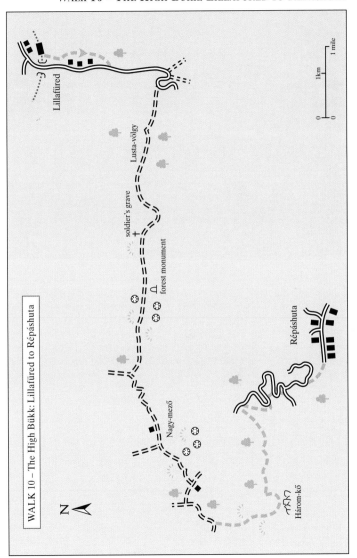

WALK 10 – The High Bükk: Lillafüred to Répáshuta

Lillafüred

Lusta-völgy

soldier's grave

forest monument

Nagy-mező

Répáshuta

Három-kő

N

0   1km

0   1 mile

*Három-kő,
Bükk-fennsík*

Starting at **Lillafüred** forest railway station head straight for the park passing a buffet bar and tables. Look for the red waymarks on the trees guiding the route left and across a wooden bridge. On the other side climb the steps into the woods. Stay on the uphill path and bear right above a house, eventually passing some snack bars or ice cream parlours. Cross the car park and head left to gain the walled zigzagging trail climbing the hill. The trail contours right passing through a little tunnel. At the fork stay on the red waymarks, but after the outdoor chapel take the path descending to the main road.

Follow the road left for about 15 minutes. After a picnic spot the road snakes uphill forming a hairpin bend. Ignore the first two exits left but turn off at an asphalt forest track with a gate and a national park sign for the National Blue Route. The road ascends the densely forested Lusta-völgy (Lazy Valley) and it is quite some time before it levels out. At a meadow look for the **soldier's grave** on the right. The road, still asphalt, continues to wind around a landscape of grassy meadows, woodland edge and sink-holes. The **forest workers' monument**, set at the bottom of one of the sink-holes, is passed on the left. At a junction stay on the road. At the next junction and picnic site turn left as indicated by the signpost for Szilvásvárad. Stay on the asphalt road rather than attempt to find the criss-crossing green-waymarked trail marked on the map unless it helps save time. The road passes an open area for storing timber and an old ski lodge. At the next fork keep left and the road comes to the open country, sink-holes and juniper trees of **Nagy-mező**.

Follow the road round and it re-enters the forest. At the next junction there is an old forest guardhouse. Turn right, but ignore the next turn-off. At the next important junction pick up the blue waymarks left, passing a rain shelter and picnic tables with rolling meadow beyond. A few minutes later the blue waymarks indicate a rough trail leaving left and into the woods. It is easy to go wrong here therefore concentrate on finding the blue waymarks. Pick up a footpath turning right; it begins to run parallel with the track abandoned a few minutes before. The waymarks take the path uphill along a meadow until a trail junction. Leave the National Blue Route here and follow the greens (triangle) marking a path crossing a little meadow. The path soon rises gently through hazel scrub onto the broad meadow and crags of Három-kő. Descend from the crag to **Répáshuta** following the instructions in Walk 9.

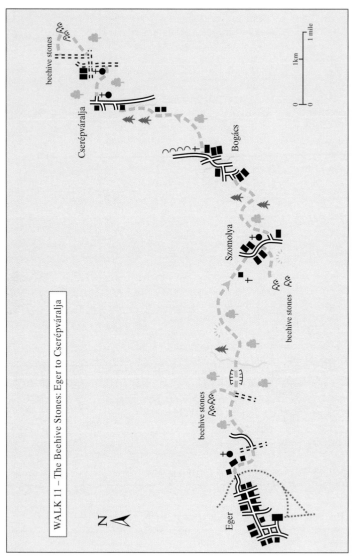

WALK 11 – The Beehive Stones: Eger to Cserépváralja

WALK 11
The Beehive Stones:
Eger to Cserépváralja

Route:	Eger – Szomolya – Bogács – Cserépváralja
Distance:	18km (11 miles)
Map:	30 Bükk (déli rész) 1:40 000
Transport:	The Bükkalja villages are well served by buses between Eger and Mezőkövesd with connections to Budapest. Note that Mezőkövesd bus station is a 20 minute walk from the railway station although there are infrequent buses.
Refreshments:	The route passes through two villages with bars, ice cream parlours and shops. Tourist-friendly Bogács offers thermal baths (*gyógyfürdő*) to relieve aches and pains.

This is an opportunity to explore the Bükkalja region in the southern Bükk and offers three short diversions to view some beehive stones. It is a long walk

Beehive stones, Szomolya

that can be completed in a day, but catch an early train from Budapest to Eger and set a decent pace. To take it easy look for accommodation on the way and complete the walk in two relaxing stages. The walk follows part of the Via ad Szomolya, a passage cut into the rhyolite which once linked the region's medieval settlements. The route is part of a long-distance walk connecting Eger with Miskolc, although the section between Cserépváralja and Miskolc is uninteresting. The southern Bükk is not a heavily walked region and at the time of writing many trails are overgrown and waymarking poor.

Diversion 1

For the first beehive stone diversion turn left at the crossroads to follow the footpath with yellow (triangle) waymarks. As the path passes through a cutting look for a wooden sign (Kaptárkő) in the trees up on the left bank. The trail disappears but follow the yellow (triangle) waymarks until it reappears to wind downhill passing a cave house on the way to the stones. Return the same way for the crossroads.

Exit **Eger**'s main railway station heading straight up the station approach road. Turn right to follow the major road. Take the second right down Hadnagy utca passing a park on the left and crossing a bridge. After a block of flats keep straight ahead until Moldári utca. Turn left; then take the first right up Merengő utca. The street soon crosses a railway and, as it leaves Eger, becomes a rough road passing a cemetery, smallholdings, orchards and a quarry. The gates of a country mansion block further progress but veer right to follow the track along the estate wall. After passing vegetable plots and weekend houses the path rises to open country and vineyards. Turn left to pass more vineyards, and at the junction of access tracks keep straight ahead and down a rough cobbled road. As the road swings left leave it for the less pronounced track going right. After a few minutes there is a fork. Turn left and try to find the yellow waymarks as the path enters woodland. At the next fork keep right to rise through the woods until reaching a clearing with a crossroads of tracks. ◀

To continue from the crossroads face the original direction of march and head for a narrow path downhill through thick woodland. The path becomes a narrow cutting with high banks and deep ruts ploughed by the wheels of ancient carts. When the path comes to a clearing it is joined from the right by a wider track. Follow it round to cross a stream. Continue straight ahead on the track uphill and back into the woods. The track is eventually flanked by the sweep of a meadow falling away to the left before arriving at a junction. Take the red-waymarked middle route into the forest. This long section eventually passes a little house with a cross and descends into the village of **Szomolya**. Turn right at the main street. ▶

To continue from Szomolya head for the church, after which the main street swings right past the cemetery and the tiny 1956 memorial park. Turn left up Dózsa György utca; it is the only street with a large wayside cross. After rising above the village and passing the last row of houses, the street ends abruptly at the forest edge. There are no waymarks, but enter the woods to locate a junction of forest paths and turn right for the well-trodden trail right passing through scrub and conifer plantation, with views north to the Bükk's long ridges.

After half an hour of mixed oak and pine forest look for the red-waymarked path turning left which descends to the outskirts of the village of **Bogács**. The track becomes a village street. Follow it downhill and at the bottom turn left, then right, for Kossuth Lajos utca. Once at the T-junction turn left to cross a bridge and at the main street turn left again. The road forks; keep right to follow Táncsics M. utca to leave the village. At the roadside cross turn right and head uphill veering right past the first of a row of wine cellars. Continue uphill to get well above the cellars then veer left. The path follows a line of crags above the scar of a speedway track, but there are excellent views of the Bükk and even the Mátra. The trail enters forest but soon comes to a rectangular clearing of cultivated land. There are no waymarks but turn right and skirt the edge of the field to its corner. Re-enter the forest to pick up a little footpath winding downhill through the woods. At the bottom join a track exiting the forest to a rough football field. Cross the field, veering left of the youth camp, and follow

Diversion 2

Follow Szomolya's main street but instead of swinging left with it towards the church, continue straight ahead and turn right for a little road climbing past a row of wine cellars. At the top there is a **Soviet Army Monument** and down at the village Szomolya's cemetery looks like a jumble of bleached bones. On the right of the monument a couple of trails begin to cross the rough pasture. Take the one flanking the orchards and vineyards. At the next fork turn left, and head for the trees. The national park sign marks where the slope drops steeply away. Descend the little path through the woods and at the bottom bear left to get the best view of the **Szomolya Beehive Stones**. Return by climbing around and to the left of the *(cont.)*

last stone to regain the meadow and backtrack to Szomolya.

the long track with a conifer plantation along its left bank. A stream and the main road can be seen through the trees on the right. When the track comes to **Cserépváralja** main street turn left. ▼

Diversion 3

Mangó-tető is the last *kaptárkő* group on the walk. Head for the centre of Cserépváralja and turn off for the twentieth-century church. Take the path winding up into the woods. Soon after the giant wine barrel cabin the trail comes to the top of the hill and open farmland. Turn left to follow a track along a fence. On the other side there is an eighteenth-century chapel. At the gates of a youth camp turn right to follow the good road, but take the next forest track left. Look out for the red-(triangle)-waymarked footpath descending right and follow it down through woods until the first beehive stone, which resembles an ice cream cone. There is another stone about 20 paces to the right. It is not as tall, but its carved compartments are more defined. To return to the village, climb the slippery path flanking the right side of the first stone. At the top follow the spine of the rock and drop down to a cutting. Turn left, passing a roadside shrine, to the youth camp road. Return to Cserépváralja the same way.

THE MÁTRA

Travelling between Budapest and Miskolc the characteristic dragon humps of the Mátra are a prominent feature. Its 40km (25 mile) ridge lies about 80km (50 miles) north-east of Budapest. Formed 13 million years ago when a chain of volcanoes erupted along a fault line stretching from the Danube to the Zemplén, the Mátra boasts Hungary's highest mountain, Kékes, which rises to 1014m (3326ft) and is recognised from a distance by its television mast. The high grassy ridges of this popular range give panoramic views down to the Great Plain or north to Slovakia. The western and eastern sections of the long high ridge (Mátrabérc) are deserted but the central section has many villages above the 800m (2600ft) contour.

History

Scythians inhabited the Mátra during the fourth century BC and the Slavs came later. With the conquering Magyars came a Turkic people called Kavars. They are thought to be the ancestors of Hungary's Palóc

Old hunters' lodge, Kaszala-kert, Mátra

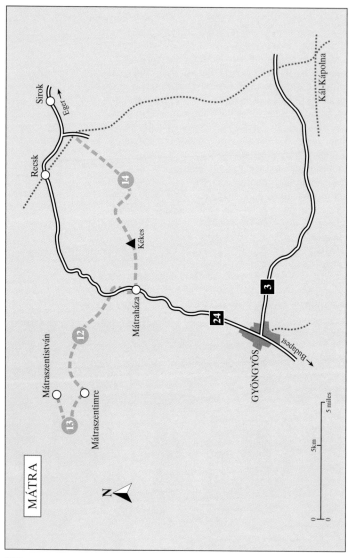

people who live in northern Hungary around the Börzsöny, Mátra and other hills. The word *palóc* is of Slav origin and means White Kun, a negative association with the raiding Cumanians, another eastern nomadic group, who settled on the Great Plain. The Kavars spoke a language that was different from early Hungarian, but after centuries of Magyarisation what remains of their speech today is the unique Palóc dialect. The hills suffered from the attention of the Hussites and also played a part in the 1514 peasant rebellion led by György Dózsa when an army recruited to fight a crusade mutinied. In the eighteenth century Slovaks settled here to work the glass foundries and a few of the names they gave to the hills and ridges have endured. Despite the assimilationist policies of past regimes a mixture of Slovak and Palóc culture survives to this day.

Recsk

Between 1950 and 1953 about 1500 political and religious dissidents and other individuals considered 'anti-social' were sent to work in the andesite quarry above the copper mining town of Recsk. The camp, discretely tucked away on the northern slope of the Mátra, was modelled on the Soviet gulag. Inmates had to survive on a thousand calories a day and many died. It was closed down and dismantled soon after Stalin's death and the area planted with trees in an effort to cover up, but in 1996 a national park of remembrance was opened as a reminder of one of Hungary's darker periods.

Routes

For the most part the walks in the guide follow sections of the 56km (35 mile) Mátrabérc túra (Mátra Ridge Race) which crosses the range from Sirok in the east to Szurdokpüspöki in the west. The race takes place on the second weekend of April starting about 6am, and the average time to complete the distance is 13 hours. Every revision of the Mátra map gives the date of the next race. The routes described below avoid the wonderfully deserted but overgrown western section between Mátrakeresztes and Szurdokpüspöki. For accessibility and refreshment facilities the central hills are excellent, although overdevelopment to cater for the tourist industry and skiing has spoiled parts of the route. Peace and quiet can be had on the eastern section of the Mátrabérc túra.

Transport

The Mátra is probably the most accessible of all the ranges. It is a lazy walker's dream as there are direct buses from Budapest Népstadion to most of the villages along the Mátrabérc and even up to the jumble of hotels, sanatorium, snack bar and television mast on the summit of Kékes. If there are no direct buses at a time to suit catch a more frequent service to Gyöngyös, from where there are local buses to the tops. Trains are more complicated: from Budapest Keleti change at Vámosgyörk for a local train to Gyöngyös. A little tourist train runs from Gyöngyös up to Mátrafüred and Lajosháza.

Accommodation

The Mátra is a popular destination and there are plenty of places to stay in and around the villages of the central region. For a little more peace and a slightly more Hungarian feel, the less developed villages of Mátraszentistván and Mátraszentimre have accommodation on offer or head for the stone-built Ágasvár *turistaház* (map reference: 102164).

Points of interest in the Mátra

Ágasvár

There is no sign of it now but a fort once stood on the summit of this prominent volcanic cone. The historical record is muddled: it was either destroyed in 1264 during the power struggle between King

Béla IV and his son István; or Austrian–Czech forces blew it up during the 1703–11 War of Independence.

Cserepes-tető
Roughly translated as Tiled Top, there was probably a watchtower here for the fort at Oroszlánvár. Its old name was Palánk-tető (Stockade Top).

Három falu temploma
The Church of the Three Villages chapel is so named because it is equidistant from the three Mátra villages.

Kékes
This is Hungary's highest mountain and its scattered boulders are the result of weathering during the Ice Age. The hostels, hotels, snack bars and litter cluttering the summit are the result of overdevelopment dating back to the 1930s. After a good fall of snow the crowds head for the Mátra and skiers race down the mountain, but few bother to walk up it. The sanatorium was a hotel in the 1930s but has been a hospital for respiratory illness since 1951. Buildings and planted trees block what should be a magnificent view, but the television tower is open to the public and has a café.

Mátra villages
With the exception of Mátraháza and Galyatető, the Mátrabérc villages were called *huta* (German for foundry). The older names are given on the map in brackets. The Hungarian composer Zoltán Kodály claimed that the Mátra was an important and unique depository of folk song and carried out some of his research here in 1905. After World War II many of the Mátra's Slovaks were repatriated to Czechoslovakia.

Oroszlánvár
Some walls and earth ramparts are still visible on this site of an old fort. Its history is unclear, but the Turks might have destroyed it in the sixteenth century.

Óvár
The name of this very prominent hill translates as Ancient Fort. From a distance the long raised line of tree crowns betrays the position of

its 1300m (1400 yard) earth rampart. Although it was originally a Bronze Age fort, it was probably recycled during the Middle Ages to form a defensive line with Ágasvár.

Sas-kő

Translated as Eagle Rock, its steep north and south walls have a Carpatho-Balkan micro-climate and provide a habitat for species of stone crop and aconite. The war memorial was erected in 1930 in memory of walkers who died in World War I.

Sirok

The substantial ruin of the fourteenth-century castle north of the village of Sirok is only just on the Mátra map. To the north of the ruins and off the map lie the interesting tufa rock formations of the Barát- és Apáca-sziklák (Monk and Nun Rocks) and Törökasztal (Turkish Table). According to legend, before the time of the Magyars a local ruler called Darnó disapproved of his daughter's love for a knight. For their disobedience the king turned the couple into the two stone columns.

Vidrócki csárda

In the nineteenth century many poor men made a living as highway robbers. During the 1848–49 Revolution one such man, Márton Vidrócki, put his ambushing skills and horsemanship to good use by leading an irregular force against the Habsburg army. Later he became a fugitive in the forests of the Mátra and the Bükk. Legend and folk song obscure the circumstances surrounding his death.

WALK 12
Mátraháza to Mátraszentistván

Route:	Mátraháza – Galyatető – Mátraszentimre – Mátraszentlászló – Mátraszentistván
Distance:	15km (9.5 miles)
Map:	14 Mátra 1:40 000
Transport:	Frequent local buses between the villages and back to Gyöngyös with one service direct to Budapest. The route never strays far from the main road and there are plenty of bus stops.
Refreshments:	No shortage of snack bars, pubs and restaurants along the way.

A fairly long but easy walk linking the Mátra villages on good forest trails and broad ridge paths with plenty of viewpoints. This is easily a day's walk with some time to relax at Mátraszentistván before catching a bus back to Gyöngyös or Budapest.

Starting at the bus company offices in Mátraháza turn left past the restaurant and snack bar and follow the wall to the red-, yellow- and blue-waymarked path down into the woods. The path undulates around a forested valley and eventually rises to regain the main road at a bus shelter. At the other side is the Vörösmarty Fogadó; cross the road and turn left. Pick up a blue- and red-waymarked path parallel with, but slightly back from, the main road. At a road junction cross left and then turn right for the blue-(+)-waymarked path ascending the steep hill to the Kós Károly look-out tower. Do not bother to climb the tower anticipating a good view; the surrounding trees are now taller than the observation platform.

Continue to follow the blue (+) waymarks along the broad forested shoulder passing the Bagoly-kő

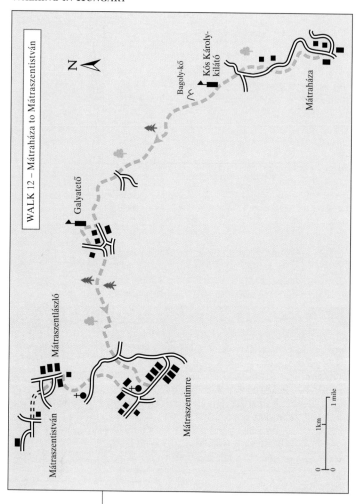

WALK 12 – Mátraháza to Mátraszentistván

N

Mátraszentistván

Mátraszentlászló

Galyatető

Bagoly-kő

Kós Károly-kilátó

Mátraháza

Mátraszentimre

0   1km
0   1 mile

(Owl Rock) outcrop with views down to the village of
Parádsasvár. The track eventually veers away from
the main road and passes a stand of conifers. Follow
the track around as it passes through woodland

before coming to an open area used as a car park. From here there is a good view down the eastern slopes. Join the main road, but at the wooden sign for Rudolftanya turn right for the red-(+)-waymarked path entering the woods. This good track passes through managed forest. Stay on the waymarks until the track exits the woods at an area of scattered trees. Follow the track straight up to a car park and into the main square of Galyatető. Over to the left is a former trade union hostel, now a hotel called the Galyatető Nagyszálló, but before that turn right to ascend a few steps onto a surfaced path, past a snack bar and WC towards Galyatető's wooded hilltop.

The hill is over 960m (3150ft) high, but it is a disappointing summit and the view from the look-out tower is not worth the climb, so turn left, descending the footpath to a road. There is a campsite below the road which swings left then right to the forest edge where it becomes a hard-packed trail undulating through conifer woods. After the gates of the observatory the path joins a straight track. Turn right, but

Ágasvár walking hostel

123

leave the path quickly at the first turning left and pick up the red waymarks. As it descends through mature forest the track passes a concrete bunker and comes to the main road and a bus shelter. Cross straight over the road passing the picnic area and pick up the red waymarks for a track heading straight up and over the tree-covered Darázs-hegy (Wasp Hill). On the other side the track descends into Mátraszentimre. At the little square and bus stop turn right along the street until the church and crossroads.

Turn right and follow the street to the end. After the last house a rough dirt track takes over. Turn left and downhill for the blue-(+)-waymarked route descending into mature woodland. When the route leaves the main track stay on the same waymarks to rise right, eventually winding around the valley and ascending to the main road. Cross the road and pick up the rough track on the other side traversing uphill and left through the woods to **Három falu temploma**. Pass the church and continue on the lane (Fenyves utca) and at the hostel (*üdülő*) swing left to follow the street (Kossuth Lajos utca) down to the village of Mátraszentlászló. Continue downhill passing a house with the sign *Kézművesek – Kiállítás* (pottery exhibition) and a bell tower. Turn left along Julius Fucik utca as indicated by the blue waymarks but leave the street soon after turning right on a little path across some grass. Cross the main road to a rough road picking up the blue waymarks. After a row of holiday cottages and workers' hostels the road enters Mátraszentistván. Follow the street down to a crossroads. The **Vidrócki csárda** is on the left.

WALK 13
Ágasvár and Csörgő-patak

Route:	Mátraszentistván – Ágasvár – Csörgő-patak – Mátraszentimre
Distance:	9km (5.5 miles)
Map:	14 Mátra 1:40 000
Transport:	Frequent local buses between the villages and back to Gyöngyös with one service direct to Budapest.
Refreshments:	No shortage of snack bars, pubs and restaurants in the villages. The first building at Ágasvár turistaház is the hostel canteen where passing walkers can buy refreshments.

This circular walk is blessed with a gentle trail contouring the wooded Sztremina ridge and volcanic cone of Ágasvár before descending a long valley through which the Csörgő-patak flows. The path follows the stream bank with its old mill and glass-foundry ruins. It will be necessary to cross the stream several times, and after heavy rain or a spring thaw it rises above the stepping-stones so expect wet feet.

Starting at the bus stop in front of **Vidrócki csárda** in Mátraszentistván head straight ahead to follow the steep downhill street. Take the first turning right on the street called Virág utca. After a guesthouse it swings left and past the Hotel Jäger after which it leaves the village and becomes a rough track. Eventually the route becomes a pleasant grassy trail with a view of **Három falu temploma** above the ski slope across the valley on the left. Keep to the blue waymarks as the trail crosses two tracks and rises through woodland contouring the Sztremina ridge until Ágasvár walkers' hostel and the hill of **Óvár** come into view. ▶

Diversion
On the way to Ágasvár hostel a blue-(triangle)-waymarked path leaves the main route to traverse up to the top of Ágasvár. There are two good views: the first is from its flat summit; and the second from the rock outcrop encountered on the descent to the hostel.

125

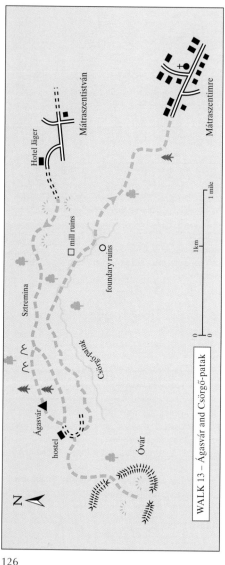

WALK 13 – Ágasvár and Csörgő-patak

After Ágasvár hostel turn off on the first little path (red and green waymarks) descending left to the access road. Turn left along the road for a short while before turning right on the red- and green-(square)-waymarked path descending through the trees. Stay on the waymarked path as it contours and undulates through forest and around the slope. After a while the red route drops away to the right, but continue straight ahead on the green (square) track which eventually descends to the Csörgő-patak. Follow the burn upstream. It will be necessary to cross it twice, and on the way the red (L) path offers a short diversion to the ruins of the old mill at Csörgőmalom. Continue along the green (square) route until the stream bifurcates. Cross both tributaries. On the other side there is a clearing, and down to the right lie the ruins of the old glass foundry. To continue, turn left and climb the path up into the forest. Cross over a wide track

and pick up the continuation of the green (square) route climbing a steep wooded spur. A conifer plantation is passed, and after some holiday cottages the track enters the village of Mátraszentimre.

Csörgő-patak-völgy

WALK 14
The Mátra ridge way (east section)

This section of the Mátrabérc túra descends to Sirok. According to tradition the route begins at Sirok and climbs to Kékes. An even lazier option is to get the bus all the way up to Kékes and start from there. Hard-packed trails wind along ridges and forested spurs and there are a few rocky outcrops with good views, most notably at Gazos-kő. Some narrowing of the path and loose stones on traverses require care. Waymarking (this is a section of the National Blue Route) is good at the beginning but soon deteriorates. A long walk, but it is still possible to treat it as a day trip from Budapest.

Route:	Mátraháza – Sas-kő – Oroszlánvár – Gazos-kő – Sirok
Distance:	23km (14 miles)
Map:	14 Mátra 1:40 000
Transport:	Buses to Mátraháza from Budapest Népstadion. At Sirok railway there are infrequent local trains to Kál-Kápolna for the main Miskolc–Budapest line. Do not get to Sirok late as the last train will leave you stuck in Hatvan with no connections to Budapest. If all the accommodation in Sirok is full there are buses to Gyöngyös with later connections to Budapest.
Refreshments:	None, and there is no buffet at Sirok railway halt. If taking the diversion up to Kékes summit there are plenty of bars and restaurants to delay the start.

Diversion

Should you insist on walking up to the summit of Hungary's rather disappointing highest mountain, Kékes, the quickest way (without wheels) is straight up the ski-run (but not in winter!). At the top turn left to find the summit rock painted in red, white and green, the colours of the Hungarian flag. To pick up the continuation of the route face the television mast, turn left, then right to pass a snack bar and descend through the woods to a broad and grassy ridge.

At Mátraháza bus company offices turn right and around the corner of the building. Cross over the road and take the road signposted to Kékestető. As the road begins its hairpin bend up to the summit take a track leaving left. After passing a little bench and wooden shelter the track merges with the run-out of a long grassy ski slope. ◀

If avoiding Kékes climb the ski slope for a few minutes before turning left on the blue (+) track to contour the forested hill with mossy boulders. After passing under a ski-jump and through a clearing with a boulder field there is a path junction. Continue straight ahead now on the yellow-(+)-waymarked trail. At a small clearing with a crossroads ascend the blue (+) path traversing up to the right. At the top it joins the broad grassy ridge of the Mátrabérc. Turn left along the blue-waymarked route passing rock outcrops and a wooden cross with good views to the north and west.

From here the path narrows as it follows the undulations of the ridge and comes to **Sas-kő** and a war memorial. Below and to the right there is a look-out point, although the view of the plain is marred by the smoke stacks of a power station which, during Communism, was named after the astronaut Yuri

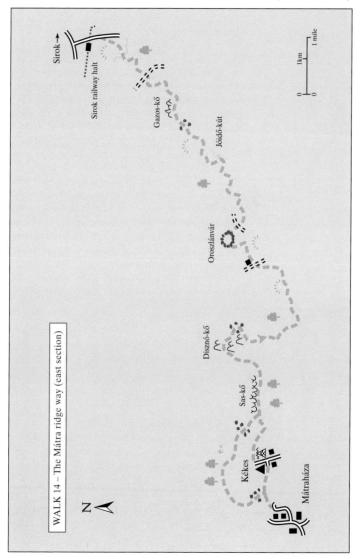

WALK 14 – The Mátra ridge way (east section)

129

Gagarin. Return to the blue waymarks to contour the north (left) slope of the ridge. After crossing over the spur at Disznó-kő (Pig Rock) the waymarked path veers around the other side, switching back on itself to give views of the pyramid-shaped **Cserepes-tető**. The narrow path continues to contour before dropping to join a forest track coming up from the left. There is a T-junction, but ignore the misleading green route dropping left and head for the gate on the other side. Climb the bank to the left and pick up the path following the fence. The path eventually swings away from the fence and around Mraznica-tető. On the other side of the hill the waymarked path briefly joins a track until turning left and into the woods, after which it widens to become a forest track. Look out for a hardly discernible minor trail descending left. It runs parallel with a forest service road before climbing over a small spur. On the other side the path arrives at a clearing with a picnic site.

Galyatető from Sas-kő

Head straight up the next hill by following the fence. Descending the other side, the footpath

becomes steeper and skirts an old conifer plantation. At the bottom cross the next forest track and
pass to the right of the old hunter's lodge picking up
the stony footpath contouring Cserepes-tető. At an
old fence the narrow path descends through patches
of beech scrub with scattered trees. Veer right at the
clearing and then left on a footpath along a fence
and through more scrub. At a clearing the path
approaches another fence: turn right to ascend the
spur through a corridor of fences to the summit of
Oroszlánvár. The remains of the circular castle wall
are still visible; follow it around left to a fence leaving no option now but to take the trail dropping
steeply left. At the bottom is a saddle with electricity
pylons called Domoszlói-kapu.

The waymarking is poor from here, but cross the
rough access road and take the middle track of three
to veer left and uphill. Turn left and, at the fence follow it, up the next spur. As the route approaches the
top, pick up the path dropping right and back into the
woods. At the bottom turn left through a gate. The
track passes through a clearing but do not get too far
ahead; take the barely noticeable little footpath left
towards the woods. At the trees the blue waymarks
reappear, guiding the route uphill. On the other side
the track descends and two fence-ladders have to be
climbed. At the good track (combined blue and yellow route) turn left, passing Jóidő-kút (Good
Weather Spring). There is one more ladder to climb,
after which the trail forks. The yellow route leaves
left but keep to the blue waymarked track swinging
right. At the next forest clearing leave the track to
veer left across the meadow and enter the woods.
Find the blue waymarks for the stony path climbing
steep Cseresznyés-tető (Cherry Top). The path now
follows a long wooded shoulder with deep gullies
falling away on the left. The next clearing with a
grassy patch and bushes is probably Gazos-kő
(Weedy Stone) outcrop. If in doubt its name is
painted in blue on the rock.

Admire the last good view of the walk before continuing along the narrowing trail to pass clumps of hawthorn and a ruined observation tower. As the trail descends it becomes steeper. Take the next turning left and downhill on the good forest path. A welcome sight at this point is the reappearance of the blue waymarks. At the bottom of this section there is a stile. Use it to get into a fenced section of partly felled forest. Head straight downhill and at the other side cross another stile. Turn right to follow the fence. The track soon bears left into the woods and crosses over a forest track. At the next track turn right then leave left on a little trail winding downhill through oak woods. A meadow appears through the trees on the left, but continue on the trail. After a rain hut the path crosses a stream and passes briefly through the last clump of woodland and another meadow with scattered bushes until the track joins the main road. Turn left for Sirok railway halt. If going to **Sirok** village, continue straight past the halt and turn right at the road junction.

THE ZEMPLÉN

Too far from Budapest for casual tourists and bypassed by the border traffic, this is a peaceful region of forest-covered volcanoes, pretty meadows and traditional peasant houses. The Zemplén lies almost 200km (120 miles) north-east of Budapest. A block of extinct volcanoes, it spans 50km (30 miles) from the famous vineyards of Tokaj to the northern-most part of Hungary where it juts into Slovakia. The highest summit is the 895m (2936ft) Nagy-Milic, a stratovolcano formed 15 million years ago. Nagy-Péter-mennykő is less imposing at 709m (2325ft) but

Füzér Castle,
Zemplén, Walk 16

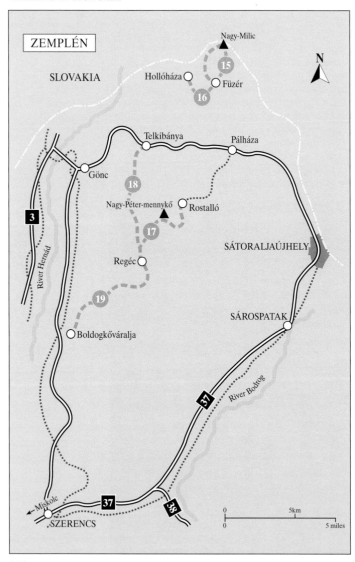

ZEMPLÉN

N

SLOVAKIA

Nagy-Milic

15

Hollóháza   Füzér

16

Telkibánya   Pálháza

Gönc

18

Nagy-Péter-mennykő   Rostalló

17

SÁTORALJAÚJHELY

Regéc

19

River Hernád

3

Boldogkőváralja

SÁROSPATAK

River Bodrog

37

Miskolc

37   38

SZERENCS

0   5km
0   5 miles

has one of the best views of the range. To the south of Nagy-Milic lies the Hegyköz basin (literally 'Between the Mountain') where most of the Zemplén villages nestle among farmland, vineyards and rough pasture. Tourist development is on the increase, but most villages have retained their charm and many of the people are descendants of eighteenth-century settlers. Smallholders here have a relaxed approach to agriculture and as a result wheat fields, road margins and ancient meadows are a haven for wild flowers including the Siberian iris.

History

Despite its tranquillity today, the Zemplén was once at the centre of Hungary's political and religious troubles. The region has endured several periods of military occupation. In the 1240s after the Mongol invasion, King Béla IV ordered the building of the Füzér, Regéc and Boldogkő strongholds. During the Middle Ages the Zemplén was an important centre for gold, silver and copper. Later, Hussites from Bohemia led by Jan Jiškra took control of the mines in order to fund their army. In the 1640s villagers fled from the Ottomans only to face looting and ill-treatment from their liberators, the Habsburg army. A combination of the unpopularity of the occupation and the region's Protestantism led to several uprisings: in 1697 angry crowds in Sátoraljaújhely market rioted and killed the Austrian and German mercenaries who regularly plundered their stalls. Many locals joined the subsequent 1703–11 War of Independence and later the 1848–49 Revolution. After the defeat of the Ottoman Empire came Slovakian, Ruthene and German settlers to work in the glass and ceramic industries. The suffix –*huta*, a feature of many Zemplén village names, refers to the glass foundries that supplied bottles for the famous Tokaj vineyards of the region. In 1894 the Phyloxera infestation destroyed the region's vines forcing many families to emigrate. Religious traditions in the

Zemplén reflect the ethnic diversity of the region. A village usually has two churches: Roman Catholic, Greek Catholic or Calvinist. Until World War II, there was a substantial Jewish minority in the Hegyköz. Today, the Roma population coexists uneasily with the other ethnic groups of the Zemplén.

Routes

The routes described in this chapter are based in the north and central Zemplén where most waymarked trails and points of interest are to be found. The walking passes through forests of ancient beech and birch, broad meadows and villages with dramatic castle ruins. The Zemplén experiences so little traffic that even road-walking is a joy in summer, when only the jangle of a corn bunting breaks the silence. The National Blue Route begins at Nagy-Milic and connects the east and west slopes in a loop. There is another path, the Rákóczi út (Rákóczi Way), which links points of interest associated with the Hungarian national hero Ferenc Rákóczi II. The routes described below follow the best sections of these long-distance paths.

Transport

The main jumping-off point is the border town of Sátoraljaújhely. Several trains a day arrive from Budapest Keleti but there is only one bus from Budapest Népstadion. Local buses depart from the front of Sátoraljaújhely railway station. Direct buses to many settlements in the north are infrequent but get as far as Pálháza for more options. The best way to the north-central Zemplén is via the little forest train from Pálháza. Villages in the western valleys have local bus services to Gönc and Novajidrány for connections to Miskolc.

Accommodation

It can take almost a whole day to get from Budapest to the walk-in points and this factor makes the

Zemplén too far for a day visit. Staying at one of the villages is a pleasant experience and it is possible to find rooms and apartments for a reasonable price during the high season, although many beds are booked up well in advance for national holidays. Pleasant Telkibánya has the most accommodation, although there are fewer tourists in Füzér. The campsite in Hollóháza offers chalets for hire. In mid-August the Zemplén Art Days are an interesting backdrop to the walking, but expect more pressure on accommodation.

Points of interest in the Zemplén

Arka

This charming village with traditional houses was a settlement as long ago as the thirteenth century. After the defeat of the Ottomans the village became a crown estate of the Habsburg Empire, and in 1650 was awarded to Slovakian Jesuits as part of the Habsburg policy to stamp out the Reformation. Judging by the Calvinist church (built in 1789) they had limited success.

Boldogkő Castle

This imposing castle managed to avoid the worst of the Ottoman wars and perhaps this is why it was given the name 'Happy Stone Castle'. Kuruc rebels occupied it in 1678, forcing the Habsburg army to destroy part of it in 1702. After the castle ceased to be of strategic importance Jesuits used the buildings to store grain. Between the 1960s and 1980s it was a walkers' hostel, but is now a museum.

Boldogkőváralja

Written records date this village to 1295, and in the eighteenth century Ruthenes and Slovaks settled here. The village museum is on the way to the castle, but visitors wishing to gain entry must contact the curator at the address on its noticeboard. With the exception of a handful of traditional houses and the Roman Catholic (1773) and Greek Catholic (1762) churches, modern development has taken its toll.

Boulder field

The local name is Kenyér-mező (bread meadow) for the area of scattered boulders formed by the cooling, fracturing and weathering of lava outflows.

Ceramic museum

In 1777 a glass foundry was founded in Hollóháza. In the 1820s gold prospectors found kaolin deposits nearby, and its ceramics industry became the second most important porcelain factory in Hungary. A famous customer was Britain's Queen Victoria. The factory was built in the 1960s to replace the original 200-year-old building that had become unsafe. The museum has an exhibition of the factory's hand-painted crockery and the adjacent factory shop is the cheapest place to buy their products.

Füzér

Many of the inhabitants of this pretty village are the descendants of Slovakian settlers. Its thatched museum is a renovated smallholder's cottage, and although its contents have been laid out in a rather contrived manner the interior gives some insight into village life. The church opposite the bus shelter was rebuilt in 1759 on the foundations of the original medieval building. A Protestant church was built at the end of the eighteenth century. Its fine ceiling paintings and carvings date back to 1832. The descent from Walk 15 passes fine examples of traditional peasant houses.

Füzér Castle

A Magyar chieftain built the first fort on this dramatic volcanic rock, but the ruin standing today was built in the thirteenth century. In 1526 Hungary's crown jewels were secured here to avoid the Ottoman plunder, but the national treasure eventually fell into Habsburg hands. During the Hungarian insurrection of 1683–99 Austrian troops destroyed most of the castle, and Leopold I awarded the estate to the loyal Károlyi family. In the 1970s villagers began restoring the ruins as part of their once-a-week voluntary work commitment. The castle hosts concerts during the Zemplén Art Days in August.

Hollóháza

There was a monastery here in the fifteenth century, but the only trace of it today is the name of the hill on which it stood (Klastrom-dűlő). Formerly two settlements, the village retains its dual character, with the best part and the oldest houses on the steep street at the north end. Landslides in recent years have caused damage to buildings and roads, forcing temporary evacuation. The village saw action during World War II and some people remember when Dózsa Gy. utca was a German artillery position. Later the Soviet Army built an underground ammunition store but neglected to inform the Hungarian authorities about its position, and live munitions continue to be unearthed. The latest find was in 2000, when grenades were uncovered during roadworks to repair landslide damage.

Lászlótanya

The National Blue Route has been diverted away from this former estate of the aristocratic Károlyi family but it is worth mentioning. During the 1956 Revolution tanks were deployed here to protect the Communist Prime Minister, Mátyás Rákosi, who often came here for the hunting.

Mogyoróska

The original Magyar settlement dates back to 1363, but in the eighteenth century Ruthenes from Trans-Carpathian Ukraine settled here. They worked as charcoal burners and up until the 1920s the Ruthenian language was widely spoken. The village church is Uniate (Greek Catholic).

Nagy-Milic

The monument on the Zemplén's highest summit marks the start of the National Blue Route. Trees obscure the view now, but previous generations could look down at neighbouring Czechoslovakia and be reminded that before 1920 the other side of the mountain was part of Hungary. Kočie (Kassa), now in Slovakia, is still considered by many to be a Hungarian town. During Communism the issue was taboo, and, although it may not be significant, until recently the north Zemplén map showed the area on the other side of the border as blank. Today's map shows Slovakian settlements and their old Hungarian names are acknowledged in brackets.

Pálháza forest train

Established in 1888 this is Hungary's oldest forest train. The single-gauge track and little diesel engines once strained under the weight of Zemplén timber but now carry tourists. Part of the 9km (5.5 mile) track passes through the Kemence-völgy nature reserve. In summer the carriages are open to the refreshing air stream, but in autumn a closed coach furnished with a wood stove keeps the autumn chill at bay. In October the train is empty apart from a few locals who use it to access the forest where they forage for acorns to feed their pigs. Services run from mid-April to mid-October and the journey to Rostalló takes about an hour.

Pusztafalu

The villagers of Pusztafalu claim descent from the Turkic Kavars who accompanied the conquering Magyars in the late ninth century. In 1526 the population converted to Protestantism, but 10 years later Tartar irregulars fighting for the Ottoman Empire destroyed the village. By 1715 the population had died out but was repopulated by Hungarian Protestants. The cemetery has examples of Protestant wooden grave posts.

Regéc

This pretty village with eighteenth-century peasant houses was destroyed during the Ottoman invasion of 1640. The Habsburg Prince Bretzenheim founded the first porcelain factory here in 1827 using clay extracted at Telkibánya. In front of the village hall there is a statue of Ferenc Rákóczi II, who led the 1703–11 War of Independence, as a child with his mother.

Regéc Castle

The Ottomans made a half-hearted attempt to destroy this magnificent castle towering above Regéc and Mogyoróska, but the credit for its destruction in 1689 goes to Habsburg troops trying to flush out Kuruc resistance to Austrian rule. It was the seat of the Protestant Rákóczi family, and Ferenc Rákóczi II spent his early childhood here. After the failure of the uprising Rákóczi fled to Rodostó in Turkey to spend the rest of his life in exile.

Telkibánya

During the Middle Ages the village was an important centre for gold, silver, copper and tin mining. At the beginning of the fifteenth century it was occupied by Jan Jiškra and his Hussite army, who exploited the mines to provide income for their military campaign. Ferenc Rákóczi II also squeezed income from the mines during the 1703–11 War of Independence against Austria. A pottery was founded in 1825 and local craftsmen and women developed a distinct decorative style using parsley and vine leaf motifs. The Protestant cemetery on the hill above the village is worth visiting for its carved wooden grave markers grouped in married-couple pairs. Visit the mining museum on the road leaving west for an interesting exhibition of local history, geology, flora and fauna.

WALK 15
Nagy-Milic and Füzér Castle

Route:	Füzér – Nagy-Milic – Bodó-rét – Füzér
Distance:	13km (8 miles)
Map:	22 Zempléni-hegység (északi-rész) 1:40 000
Transport:	Limited buses from Sátoraljaújhely; if stuck take the Hollóháza bus and get off at Füzérkomlós to pick up the blue-waymarked track for a pleasant 20 minute walk to Füzér.
Refreshments:	Half-way round the circuit there is a restaurant at Bodó-rét, and in Füzér the pub has a shaded veranda.

Füzér Castle ruin provides a dramatic backdrop to this circular route following the blue waymarks. The first half of the walk is a long ascent through forest to the wide ridge between Hungary and Slovakia. Trees obscure the view from Nagy-Milic, but the zigzagging descent offers views down to Slovakia. The half-day walk can be prolonged with a lunch at Bodó-rét restaurant. The post-prandial descent to Füzér can be taken at a relaxing pace and soon leaves the forest to cross an old orchard and meadow with grand views of the castle on the rock.

Diversion

Before embarking on the main walk it is worth taking a detour up to Füzér Castle for the excellent view. At the little saddle above the bandstand swing right and find a path with red waymarks leading to the rough stone steps up the castle rock. It is not far to the ruin, but allow an hour for the round trip.

Start at **Füzér** bus stop and face the church. Turn right along the main street passing the post office and village bar. Take the first turning right past the Protestant church and turn left at the back road to pass the thatched village museum. After leaving the village the road approaches a bandstand on a grassy slope, but before that take the little track up to the right crossing the meadow uphill towards the wooded saddle. ◀

To continue from the woods above the bandstand look for the blue waymarks among the confusion of

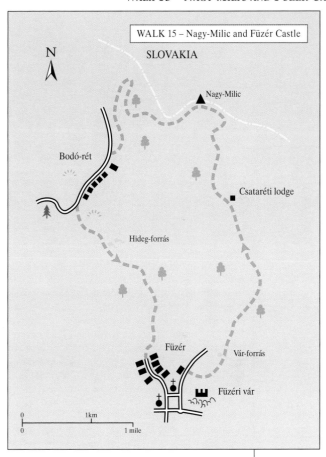

trails leading into the forest. The path comes to a spring; head uphill and to the right of it and veer left to contour the hill on a good track. After some time the track crosses a shallow stream. On the other side follow the path up the valley to Csataréti hunting lodge. From here the path rises steeply through dense woodland to a ridge where the trees thin out. Continue to

*Charcoal kiln,
Bodó-rét*

ascend and pick up evenly spaced red and white posts marking the Slovakian border and follow them for the final approach to the monument on the summit of **Nagy-Milic**. The last section is more or less level, and as a result the event is an anti-climax.

On the descent the path switches back several times giving glimpses down to the town of Košiče in Slovakia. A fence blocks the approach to **Lászlótanya**, but the blue waymarks divert the route left for a while before dropping onto an asphalt road. Turn left and Bodó-rét, with its bar and restaurant and garden tables, is soon reached.

Continue on the road past a row of holiday cottages and take the first track left across a meadow to join the blue (+) route. Follow it down and left. The track enters the forest and passes the Hideg-forrás springs and exits for the last time. The fortress soon comes into view. From here the waymarks disappear, but the stony track steadily descends through the old orchard into Füzér.

WALK 16
Hollóháza to Füzér

Route: Hollóháza – Füzér

Distance: 4km (2.5 miles)

Map: 22 Zempléni-hegység (északi rész) 1:40 000

Transport: Limited buses connect the three villages, but if it is necessary to walk back along the road there is little traffic. To get back to Budapest catch a bus to Sátoraljaújhely railway station.

Refreshments: The *italbolt* (bar) in Füzér is a good place to spend the rest of the afternoon.

This short and easy section of the long-distance Rákóczi Way is suitable for walkers who have decided to stay at Hollóháza and want to explore Füzér and other villages or perhaps to continue up to Nagy-Milic as in Walk 15. The route follows the main road until turning off, but perseverance is rewarded by a sudden exit from forest to a broad meadow and a view of Füzér Castle perched on its volcanic plug. If the day is unbearably hot, take the lazy option and spend the rest of the afternoon on the veranda of the bar in Füzér with the local men who are likely to be discussing the state of the village wells.

Starting at the **Ceramic museum** leave **Hollóháza** and head south along the quiet main road and turn left on the track with red waymarks. It is a rough vehicle track at first but soon narrows to a trail rising gently through woodland. It is not long before Füzér's fortress appears framed in the gap between the trees. Follow the track crossing the meadow heading downhill for the village. As the track approaches the first houses it becomes a rough street and crosses a little bridge. At the junction turn right

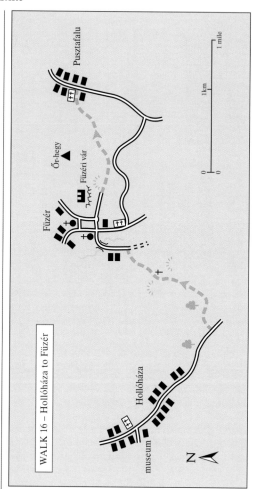

WALK 16 – Hollóháza to Füzér

Extension: Pusztafalu

Suppress your thirst and at the top of the street continue straight ahead past the bus stop up a rough road. After the last houses Füzér Castle towers above the vegetable plots on the left. There are no waymarks, but stay on the track as it skirts the forest around Őr-hegy and then descends to Pusztafalu.

to climb the steep road to the church and bus stop. Turn left for the village pub. ◀

Road to Füzér

WALK 17
Rostalló to Mogyoróska

Route:	Rostalló – István-kút – Nagy Péter-mennykő – Regéc – Mogyoróska
Distance:	15.5km (9.5 miles)
Map:	22 Zempléni-hegység (északi rész) 1:40 000
Transport:	Buses link Pálháza with Sátoraljaújhely and Füzér. Limited buses from Regéc and Mogyoróska to Novajidrány and other villages with connections to Miskolc. For a head start and to avoid a long walk-in catch the first Pálháza forest train to Rostalló. The timetable is on the reverse of the walking map.
Refreshments:	Apart from snack bars along the forest railway there is nothing until Regéc, where the shop which shares the same premises and staff as the village bar opens late and on Sundays.

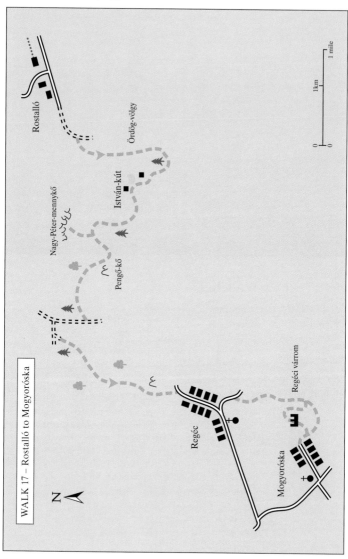

WALK 17 – Rostalló to Mogyoróska

The route crosses the Zemplén from east to west passing through old birch and beech forest. The rocky outcrop of Nagy-Péter-mennykő offers a commanding view to the north. Regéc and Mogyoróska are surrounded by open farmland which is dominated by a castle ruin on a volcanic hill. The going is easy and the waymarking generally good. If visiting in summer keep an eye out for the Siberian iris wherever woodland gives way to patches of meadow.

Starting at the Rostalló forest train terminus walk to the end of the track to an asphalt road. Turn left, then right. The buildings passed on the right are hire-only walking hostels. As the road progresses up the valley of Ördög-völgy the asphalt gives way to gravel. After a quarter of an hour the yellow-waymarked path leaves right to climb a steep bank to a forest track. Cross over and continue uphill on the waymarks but at the next track turn left. The track is now high above the valley. After passing a stand of conifers there is a

Walkers on Regéc Castle

Diversion

This short diversion to the viewpoint at Nagy-Péter-mennykő is worth the extra effort and is a pleasant spot for a refreshment break. Look for the blue (triangle) waymarks indicating a grassy path right. After crossing the meadow with scattered birch trees the trail disappears in among the beech wood, but keep to the waymarks. Reverse to the main route.

fork; turn right. This path narrows and soon breaks up, but the yellow waymarks guide the way uphill along a ditch. At the top turn right following the rough forest track until a clearing of scattered birch and pine and a junction. Veer right on the blue-waymarked track and at the national park sign take the minor track descending left through the István-kút birch woods. After 10 minutes a hunting lodge and pond are passed and then another house which is the István-kút hunting lodge. The path now rises gently through birch scrub. At the top turn left onto a stony forest track which contours a spur through pine forest. Some time after passing the firebreak with a rock the track swings left and rises to a clearing. ◀

Back at the main route turn right to continue on the blue waymarks. Follow the track over a spur to a fork and turn right. From here the track rises gently, passing a conifer wood and old beech forest. Ignore the blue (triangle) waymarks for the diversion to Pengő-kő (Clinking Stone); the view from the boulder is now obscured by trees. Stay on the broad forest track as it swings left passing through partly felled areas of forest.

At the T-junction of muddy forest tracks, turn right on the blue- and green-waymarked track. After a few minutes a crossroads of well-used forest tracks and confusing waymarks is reached. Turn left to continue on the blue waymarks, but as the track veers right turn left for another track following the edge of a conifer plantation. Over on the left there is open country with a hunting tower and a hill capped with pine trees. Apart from a few stands the area is felled plantation, but recently repainted blue waymarks guide the route to the edge of a beech forest and the steep drop-away of a slope.

Confirm that the steep cutting descending through the forest has blue waymarks before proceeding. At what seems like the bottom the going levels and there is a clearing with a crossroads of rough tracks. Turn left for the heavily rutted track descending into more forest, but follow it for only a few paces before turning right on a narrow path into the forest. Count 20 paces if not sure. Picking up the blue waymarks, the path gently descends a forested valley. After a while it passes through an area of mossy boulders and at the largest outcrop turn left across a stream. The trail is obvious from here and, as it descends, passes through a clear area affording the first glimpse of Regéc castle hill. After dropping right the trail crosses and recrosses the stream several times. Look for the blue-waymarked stones leading to **Regéc**.

Follow the village main street (Fő utca) for a while and turn left across a bridge. The road twists right, then left as it leaves the village. Turn right onto a rough track passing vegetable plots and across fallow land with scattered bushes. The track heads for the forest girding the castle hill. Once the trees are reached there are abundant waymarks and signs marked *Vár* (castle) along the track. After about 20 minutes there is a right turn for **Regéc Castle**. From here it is a good 10 minute climb to the summit and its extensive ruin with splendid views of the surrounding hills and the villages of Mogyoróska and Regéc. An alternative descent is possible by turning left down the steep red (L) waymarked track which was passed on the way up. At the bottom turn right to pass through a clearing with a wooden rain shelter. Follow the track down into **Mogyoróska**. ▶

WALK 18
Telkibánya to Regéc

Rising steadily from the village, the route follows uninteresting forest tracks at first, but once up and over the tops the trail narrows, passing through protected woodland. The long descent to Regéc on the blue waymarks follows the same route as in Walk 17. The green-waymarked section south of Telkibánya is

Alternative Route

Avoiding the slog up to the fort, there is a short cut between Regéc and Mogyoróska cutting out the main road. Instead of turning left over the bridge, continue down Regéc's long main street (Fő utca). After the last village house turn left at the roadside cross for a path. Ford the little stream and turn right to follow the overgrown track traversing uphill through the woods. The track is marked on the map but is not waymarked, and as it crosses open country with scattered bushes it begins to disappear, but bear left to skirt a wooden fence. The other side of the castle ruin is up on the left, and Mogyoróska's church spire is visible ahead. Veer left for the village.

hard to follow at times, although the waymarks for
the National Blue Route were recently repainted.

Route:	Telkibánya – Bohó-hegy – Regéc
Distance:	12km (7.5 miles)
Map:	22 Zempléni-hegység (északi rész) 1:40 000
Transport:	Although Telkibánya is in the western part of the Zemplén, the town of Gönc in the Hernád Valley is not the best approach if relying on public transport. Catch a bus from Sátoraljaújhely – the journey takes about an hour. At the end of the walk there are a few local bus services from Mogyoróska to Novajidrány and main line rail services to Miskolc.
Refreshments:	At Regéc the combined bar and grocery shop opens late and on Sundays.

Starting at the bus stop in the centre of **Telkibánya**
turn right then left down the village road called
Szabadság utca for the red- and green-waymarked
route. The road crosses a bridge and veers left uphill,
but as it veers right take the path on the left up
through the woods along the back of a cemetery. The
trail climbs a steep wooded slope, but as it approaches
a wide firebreak turn left to continue uphill on the
green-waymarked route. At a forest track follow its
contour around to the left for a while and join
another track. At a junction ignore the green (square)
turning and continue straight ahead on the main
green route. The track rises and begins to swing right.
At the fork turn left on the lesser track which rises
steeply. Veer right at a fork away from the main track
which now drops away to the left. Climb the ladder to
clear a deer fence and follow the uphill track on the
other side. After a while there is another fence but do
not climb the first ladder; turn left to follow the fence
to another ladder.

On the other side of the fence there are no waymarks, but follow the track straight ahead and at the
fork take the left to pass through a conifer plantation.

After a while the track veers right into mature pine forest and the green waymarks reappear. At the next fork turn left. Ignore the next turn-off marked by green (triangle) waymarks; it was once a good viewpoint but trees obscure it now. At a T-junction keep right, then left, climbing a steep section of track to yet another deer fence. Turn left on the narrow footpath following the fence contouring the steep hill with mossy boulders. Eventually the fence gives way. After passing a conifer plantation turn right to ascend Bohó-hegy.

There is little to see from the summit so turn left to follow the waymarks gently downhill. On the left a jumble of boulders marks where the slope drops steeply, so keep on the path, which eventually descends to a national park sign and a fence. Turn left and follow the long track passing through pine forest to a junction of deeply rutted tracks, log piles and confusing

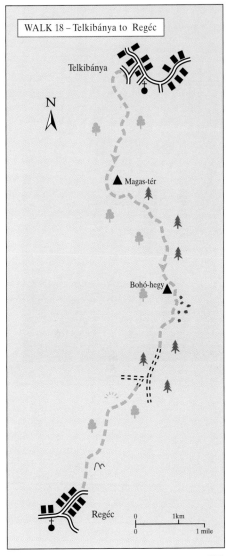

WALK 18 – Telkibánya to Regéc

Telkibánya

N

▲ Magas-tér

Bohó-hegy ▲

Regéc

0   1km

0   1 mile

Rákóczi monument, Regéc

waymarks. Do not follow the combined waymarked route dropping left but continue straight ahead, swinging right on a blue-waymarked track. As it veers right turn onto the track on the left. From here the track skirts a conifer plantation. Over on the left there is open country with a hunting tower and a hill capped with pine trees. Apart from a few stands the area is felled plantation, but recently repainted blue waymarks guide the route to the edge of a beech forest and the steep drop-away of a slope.

Confirm that the steep cutting descending through the forest has blue waymarks before proceeding. At what seems like the bottom the going levels and there is a clearing with a crossroads of rough tracks. Turn left for the heavily-rutted track descending into more forest, but follow it for only a few paces before turning right on a narrow path into the forest. Count 20 paces if not sure. Picking up the blue waymarks, the path gently descends a forested valley. After a while it passes through an area of mossy boulders, and at the largest outcrop turn left across a stream. The trail is obvious from here and as it descends passes through a clear area affording the first glimpse of Regéc castle hill. After dropping right the trail crosses and recrosses the stream several times. Look for the blue-waymarked stones leading to **Regéc**.

WALK 19
Mogyoróska to Boldogkőváralja

Route:	Mogyoróska – Arka – Boldogkőváralja – Boldogkő Castle
Distance:	10km (6 miles)
Map:	22 Zempléni-hegység (északi rész) 1:40 000
Transport:	There are limited buses linking Boldogkőváralja with Encs, Gönc, Abaújkér and Abaújszántó for connections to Miskolc and Budapest. Boldogkőváralja railway halt is almost 3km (2 miles) away from the village and services are infrequent.
Refreshments:	None until Arka and Boldogkőváralja. Note that there is no buffet bar at Boldogkőváralja railway halt.

It takes only a couple of hours to complete this walk linking Mogyoróska and Boldogkőváralja. The pretty village of Arka and the dramatic castle and museum of Boldogkő add historical interest. The fit walker may wish to turn this section into a continuation of the Rostalló to Mogyoróska route (Walk 17) but research the public transport thoroughly or arrange accommodation. The blue-waymarked trail is good but there is one awkward nettle patch. Until it is revised, the map may still show the old Blue Route going up to the hill with a 299m spot height between Arka and Boldogkőváralja. Do not attempt to climb it as the summit is overgrown and the tower, which promises a good view of the castle, is in ruins. The alternative route to Boldogkőváralja follows a minor road with little traffic.

At **Mogyoróska** church there is a T-junction. Turn right and then left down what is a continuation of the village main street (Fő utca). The road descends gently, but before the last house look for a little footpath on the right dropping into a meadow. Head for the

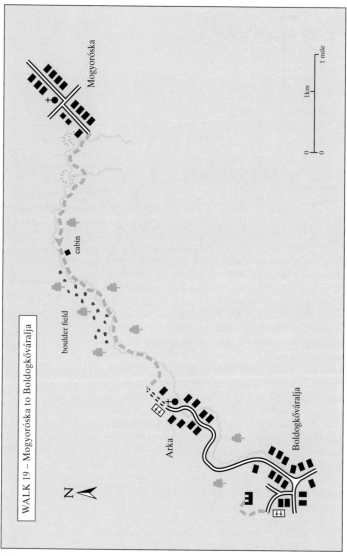

WALK 19 – Mogyoróska to Boldogkőváralja

N

Mogyoróska

cabin

boulder field

Arka

Boldogkőváralja

0   1km
0   1 mile

stream and cross it to pick up the blue-waymarked trail. Turn right, and at the next fork take the more distinct track left. The path hugs a rocky bank as it swings left, soon narrowing, and crosses another stream and a meadow before joining another track. At the next fork take the grassy track left into the trees. After passing a cabin and an old well the path narrows through a nettle patch and crosses a rickety bridge. From here the **boulder field** is visible up on the right slope of the valley. The path crosses the stream several times on the way before settling for the right bank to rise up through bushes and wild plum trees and open country. After following a fence of an orchard the path comes to a junction. Turn left for **Arka**. After the village follow the main road to **Boldogkőváralja**. At the main street turn right past the bar. For **Boldogkő Castle** take the next right up a rough village street bearing left at the fork. After the cemetery there is a trail up to the castle.

Horse and cart, Mogyoróska

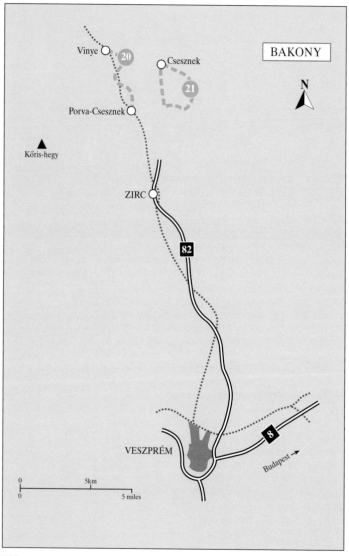

WALKS IN
TRANSDANUBIA

THE BAKONY

'I have never seen such a forest more picturesquely intermingled with open views and cultivated lands', wrote Richard Bright in 1818, the English doctor better known for his research into renal disease. He was an adventurous traveller and spent several months in Austria and Hungary and wrote an encyclopaedic account of his journeys, *Travels from Vienna through Lower Hungary*. The Bakony's low plateau is situated 60km (37 miles) to the south-west of Budapest and stretches from the town of Mór at its north-east edge to Lake Balaton in the south. Two types of countryside dominate: hilly woodland with deep, cool and thickly forested valleys pungent with wild garlic; and open, dry windy plateau where fields of wheat, sunflowers and potatoes are interspersed with bushy downland and woods. The average height is between 400m and 500m (1300–1600ft) although its highest point, Kőris-hegy in the north, is 709m (2325ft). The Tés plateau to the east of Zirc is karstic, but to compensate for the lack of water power the inhabitants built windmills to harness the strong winds characteristic of the region.

Karl Marx, Veszprém railway buffet

History

Illyrians settled here, and deep in the rarely visited woods of Százhalom north of Bakonybél the 226 tumuli they left behind lend an eerie atmosphere to the forest. The Bakony witnessed an important moment in Hungarian history in AD 997 when King Stephen I crushed a rebellion led by his uncle, Koppány, the pagan chieftain. The event ensured Hungary's transformation into a Christian kingdom. Béla III founded the town of Zirc in the centre of the range, and the French Cistercian monks he invited to settle built a monastery. From 1720 Germans and Slovaks settled in the forests to work the glass foundries and produce wooden tools. In 1776 the official language of the village of Porva was German, and although few Bakony people speak German today many villagers continue to identify themselves as 'Swabians'. The hills were a favourite haunt for highwaymen (*betyár*), who are celebrated in popular ballads, but the Bakony's most famous fugitive was Ferenc Szálasi, leader of Hungary's Fascist party, the Arrow Cross, who hid here from the advancing Red Army at the end of World War II.

Routes

Of all Hungary's walking areas the Bakony is the most frustrating as many of its routes are poorly waymarked, overgrown or follow busy main roads. This is rather unfortunate as the people who inhabit the neat little villages on the plateau are friendly. Bakonybél, cradled in wooded hills, is a more peaceful base than Zirc, but apart from the short walk following green waymarks to the grave mounds at Százhalom there is little walking interest. The highest summit, Kőris-hegy, is blighted by an ugly radar station and not worth the bramble-bashing trip. Having said all that Hungarians are becoming more interested in walking so waymarking and path maintenance are likely to improve. The two short walks described below are good outings.

Transport

Trains leave from Budapest Déli. Change at Veszprém for Zirc. From Zirc railway station it is a long trek to the town's main square and bus station. Long-distance buses for the Bakony depart from Budapest Népliget.

Accommodation

The area is a popular destination for families and parties of children, and in summer there is quite a holiday atmosphere on the trains lumbering through the Cuha Valley, but there is a lot of pressure on accommodation. Hotels, guesthouses and private rooms are in abundance; ask at the Zirc branch of Tourinform for a list. A room in a private house is often better value than any establishment calling itself a *turistaszálló* or *üdülő*, which is likely to be full of noisy children. There is a campsite in the village of Kardosrét to the north of Zirc and camping places in Csesznek and Bakonybél. To stay at the Vasutas *turistaház* (railway hostel) at Porva-Csesznek station in Cuha Valley, ask at the railway buffet.

Points of interest in the Bakony

Csesznek Castle

The important Csák clan built this castle in 1263. In 1552 the Ottomans besieged it several times without success. In 1594 the captain surrendered the castle after suffering a crisis of confidence when news arrived that the town of Győr had been taken. It saw shots fired in anger during the anti-Habsburg wars of liberation but today's ruins are a result of an earthquake and a fire caused by a lightning strike.

Vasutas hostel

Opposite the railway buffet in the cool shade of tall pine trees this hostel is a survival of socialist paternalism and is one of many establishments set up for the exclusive use of railway employees and their families. It still functions as a hostel and the bed linen bears the stamp of the former Hungarian Socialist Workers Party School. Make enquiries at the railway buffet.

WALK 20
Cuha Valley

Route:	Vinye – Cuha-völgy – Porva-Csesznek railway halt
Distance:	5km (3 miles)
Map:	2 Bakony (északi rész) 1:40 000
Transport:	Trains from Zirc
Refreshments:	There are snack bars and hostels at Vinye, but the buffet at Porva-Csesznek railway halt is a peaceful spot between trains.

Vasutas hostel, Cuha Valley

Bakony's tourist brochures extol the beauty of the Cuha Valley, but the entire walk from Zirc in the south to Bakonyszentlászló in the north is not worth the effort. The first section follows an unpleasant

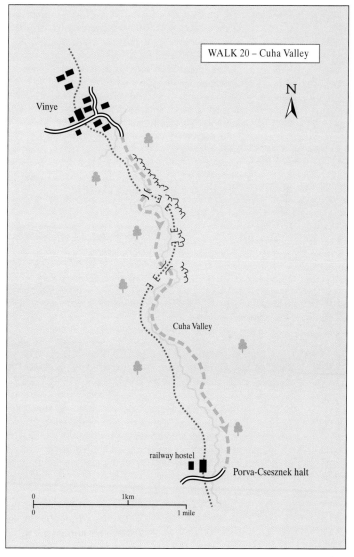

WALK 20 – Cuha Valley

N

Vinye

Cuha Valley

railway hostel

Porva-Csesznek halt

| 0 | | 1km | |
| 0 | | | 1 mile |

163

busy main road carrying heavy lorry traffic. The northern section near Bakonyszentlászló is diverted onto a road covered in red dust from mining lorries. The middle section described below is rather short and undemanding but is a pleasant half-day out including travelling.

Starting at the dilapidated Vinye railway halt follow the road past the timber yards towards a group of buildings. After veering right into the woods the road ends at a barrier to pick up the red-waymarked footpath along the stream. From here it is a straight-forward walk upstream until the Porva-Csesznek railway halt and the **Vasutas hostel**.

WALK 21
Ördög-árok

Route:	Csesznek – Ördög-árok – Kő-árok – Csesznek
Distance:	12km (7.5 miles)
Map:	2 Bakony (északi rész) 1:40 000
Transport:	Bus services between Zirc and Csesznek
Refreshments:	Shops, bars and a restaurant at Csesznek

The Bakony has many deep valleys and gorges cut into its plateau with plenty of interest for botanists, but few are worth walking for their own sake. The Ördög- and Kő-árok are exceptions and provide a good day's walking. The start and finish pass through farmland but there is mature forest most of the way. The crumbling banks and a tiny scramble up the broken iron ladder at Gizella-átjáró are not difficult, but the walk is probably not suitable for people who are anxious about these things. Drier Kő-árok with its towering beech trees and high walls is grander than

Ördög-árok. The route is probably best avoided after several days of heavy rain. To round off the walk visit the castle ruin in Csesznek.

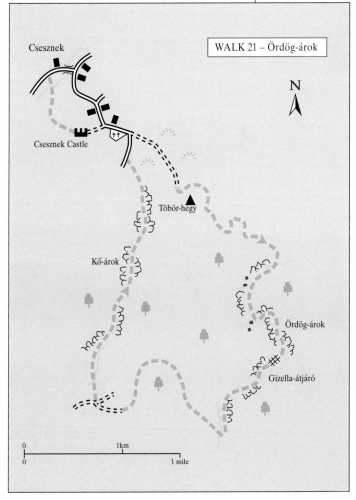

WALK 21 – Ördög-árok

N

Csesznek

Csesznek Castle

Töbör-hegy

Kő-árok

Ördög-árok

Gizella-átjáró

0   1km
0   1 mile

Find the village street called Vasút út and pick up a little footpath and steps to a tiny footbridge. On the other side of the stream ascend to the vegetable plots from where there is a good view of **Csesznek Castle**. Veer to the right and enter the woods. At first the narrow path is a bit exposed as it follows a narrow ledge, but soon veers away from the gully climbing left and up a wooded spur. Ignore the red (+) waymarks and take the green (triangle) route. If you miss the waymarks, follow the hill straight up through the trees to the old Jewish cemetery and veer left along the path until it joins the rough castle track. To visit the ruins, turn right. If saving the ruins for the return journey, turn left and follow the castle road down to Vár út and turn right to follow the road out of the village.

As the main road passes the cemetery take the red-waymarked track leaving left. After passing through open farmland the track comes to a fork; take the right branch with an old hunting hide. After entering the forest there is a junction of tracks. Turn left to contour the wooded hill called Töbör-hegy. Fifteen minutes later at the next junction keep left

The Bakony plateau

on the red waymarks. The route is well waymarked from here but beware of being side-tracked. Eventually the route crosses a forest break with pylons. Once back in the forest at the other side the path joins a forest track. Follow it downhill and at the confusing junction veer left, then turn right, to join another downhill track. At the bottom there is a stream and the mouth of Ördög-árok. Turn right to follow the gully upstream as it narrows to a deep gorge with boulders and caves. After the broken ladder at Gizella-átjáró (Gizella was the wife of King Stephen I) the gully gradually broadens to a valley. At the top continue along the stream to a junction of waymarked routes.

Turn right for the green- and red-(square)-waymarked path which soon leaves the forest to cross scrub and meadow and passes under electric pylons. The path enters more trees and from here there is a long forest walk. Avoid confusing side tracks by keeping to the green and red (square) waymarks.

When the track descends to a major junction of forest tracks head for the other side picking up the green waymarks indicating a footpath cutting through the trees and bushes on the right. A small house just visible on the left (not on the map) is passed and from here the route is a straightforward descent of the Kő-árok Valley. At the bottom the path veers left and rises a little to open farmland. Follow the track down to the main road where Csesznek Castle comes into view. At the main road turn right, and after a while the cemetery appears as the road enters Csesznek.

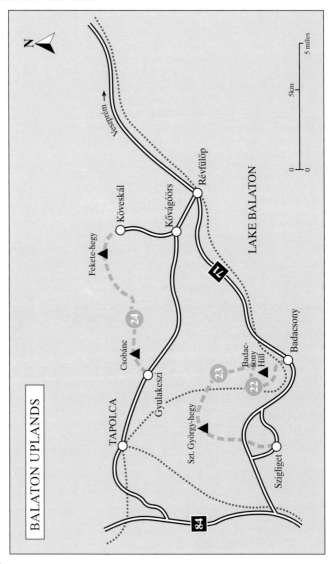

THE BALATON UPLANDS

Of all the destinations in Hungary, Lake Balaton with its beach resorts, hillside vineyards, orchards and traditional houses is probably the most popular destination for foreign tourists. Its east shore and conurbation of seaside towns has little walking interest, but on the other side lie the Balaton Highlands (Balaton-felvidék), an escarpment of the Bakony, and the buttes of the Badacsony. The latter were formed 10 million years ago when the Pannonian Basin was a sea and its deep layer of sediment was fractured by submerged volcanic eruptions. After the sea receded the exposed sediments were eroded leaving behind the harder basalt columns. The summits mark the level of the original sea bed, thus the Hungarian name *tanúhegyek* (witness mountains). The summits are not high – Badacsony is only 437m (1433ft) – but the broad flat farmland of the basin called the Káli-medence and the sweep of Lake Balaton give the hills a dramatic aspect.

Villager and Csobánc, Balaton Uplands

History

In the first century BC Roman legions arrived at the Carpathian Basin, and after defeating the last free Celtic tribes they incorporated the area west of the Danube into the Empire and called it Pannonia. Under Roman rule this frontier province enjoyed a period of stability, prosperity, agricultural innovation and urban development. The Romans enjoyed the mild climate and thermal springs, anticipating its popularity as a future tourist resort. By the fourth century AD the citizens of Pannonia had abandoned their pagan cults for Christianity, pre-dating Saint Stephen's efforts to convert the early Hungarians. Many place-names preserve the memory of the first Magyar camps of the Káli clan who settled the low land between the hills.

Today the hills are dotted with weekend cottages and wine bars. During Communism it was a favourite resort for East Germans who came here to meet their West German relatives and perhaps plan their defection to the West. The locals who did well out of the demand for accommodation and Hungary's relaxed version of Communism are known as the Zimmer Frei Mafia.

The quintessential Lake Balaton scene popular with Hungarian wine advertisements and tourist brochures is the flat-topped plateau of Badacsony Hill, but from the beginning of the twentieth century it was stripped of basalt to feed Hungary's rapidly growing cities. Initially the stone was extracted manually and the quarrymen lived a communal existence in the Felsőkolónia cottages on Badacsony's east slope. Conservationists objected to the destruction of the basalt columns. In the 1950s operations ceased as a result of commercial pressures and an effort was made to rectify the environmental damage. The clumps of pine trees growing around the bottom of the old quarries are the result of a reforestation programme started in 1954.

Routes

Hungarians who can still afford the inflated prices come to Lake Balaton to swim in its warm shallow waters, lie on its pay-as-you-enter beaches and frequent its night clubs, but rarely walk along its many trails. The network of waymarked paths around the villages of the Balaton Uplands is quite extensive but the walks in the guide are concentrated around the Badacsony buttes and the Káli-medence. Information boards *en route* interpret the history and geology of the region in English. Footpaths are usually hard-packed, and waymarks well maintained, although there are a couple of stretches of asphalt to connect the remnant hills. Wine cellars and bars waylay the visitor who prefers a more relaxed approach to walking.

Transport

Frequent rail services from Budapest Déli connect the city with the string of resorts along the western shore of Lake Balaton, but try to avoid the slow (*személy*) trains that stop at every station. A few fast trains go direct to Lake Balaton but it might be necessary to change at Székesfehérvár. Long-distance buses leave from Budapest Népliget, and there are local services between Tapolca and Révfülöp connecting the villages in the Káli-medence. In summer passenger ferries sail frequently between many shore towns, and a steam train for tourists runs between Keszthely and Tapolca.

Accommodation

There is no shortage of accommodation as plenty of houses advertise their spare rooms and apartments, although prices are high in this popular region. Campsites are situated along the lake shore with easy access to the hills (and the beach), but these are also rather expensive compared to other regions of Hungary. The season is very short; if you come before June and after August do not expect many places to be open, although this state of affairs will probably change in the future. Rodostó-ház, the former hostel on Badacsony Hill, is now a private residence, but the *turistaház* on Szt.György-hegy is available for pre-booked parties.

Points of interest in the Balaton Uplands

Basalt columns

These 30m (100ft) high basalt columns were formed from rapidly cooled lava of submerged volcanoes. For a better view, get above the columns and then take one of the footpaths off to the left or right.

Csobánc

'…the ascent offers a series of the most beautiful views…the prospect is varied by other insulated mountains, and the fine extent of the Balaton lake', remarked Doctor Richard Bright after climbing this hill. That was in 1818, but its tree-less summit still offers stunning views of the Káli-medence and Lake Balaton. In 1561 the Ottomans attacked the fort, and its fate was finally decided by a duel between the leaders of both sides. In 1707 the fort faced another challenge when 60 Hungarian rebels held it against 1500 Habsburg troops.

Korkovány

According to tradition the name comes from the German expression *Kar kein Wein*, the first words of the eighteenth-century German wine merchants when they tried the poorer quality wine of Badacsony's northern slope.

Kőtenger

The information board explains the origins of these boulder fields that were once scattered all over the Káli-medence.

Lake Balaton

Here are a few facts to ponder while resting on one of the viewpoints on Badacsony, Szt.György-hegy or Csobánc. At 77km (48 miles) long and a bit over 14km (9 miles) at its widest point, this is Central Europe's largest stretch of fresh water. A relic of the Pleistocene Age, the lake was formed when the Pannonian Sea receded and left some of its water to stagnate in a trench created by a geological fault. The water is not very deep and reaches its maximum of 11m (35ft) at the tip of the Tihany peninsula. Fortunately for Hungary the plan to drain it was never realised because after the Treaty of Trianon Hungary lost its only coast (now Croatia, Slovenia and part of Italy). Lake Balaton is now known as Hungary's sea. Commercial fishing has reduced over the decades and only a few operators can make a living from the lake today.

Lengyel Chapel

The Lengyel family built this pretty chapel in 1775. The door is left open for tourists to peer through a gate at the elaborately carved interior and Baroque statues of various saints.

Rodostó-ház

Built in 1935 complete with traditional thatched roof, the building was a walking hostel but it is now private property. It is named after the Turkish town where Ferenc Rákóczi II, the leader of the failed War of Independence, spent the rest of his life in exile. The blue way-marks turning left down a steep path come to the 464 steps of the Bujdosók lépcsője, which commemorate the exiles of 1711. The plaques at the top of the steps mention walkers who have completed the National Blue Route and famous Hungarian mountaineers who climbed in the Tatras.

Szegedi Róza-ház

The poet Sándor Kisfaludy often visited the area and fell in love with 19-year-old Róza Szegedi whose father owned this wine press, which is now a museum. Their love was a recurring theme throughout Kisfaludy's romantic poetry. Just as sweet but perhaps not so sickly, Róza's invention, the wine called *ürmös*, probably did more to uplift the heart. Women drank it before church so that they would be in good voice during the service. In July there is a festival in memory of Róza.

Szentbékkálla

Most regions of Hungary have some kind of women's festival where male authority is overturned. In this village the Asszony Farsang is a time when only women are allowed near the vineyards or the cellars to taste wine and the men are chased away with broomsticks.

Szigliget

Richard Bright said of the village that it was 'built with the utmost irregularity upon the side of a rocky elevation'. The place retains some of its nineteenth-century charm, and today the old women sit on the porches of their traditional thatched houses. There was probably a Roman fort on its hill, although the current castle (now a ruin) was built in 1262. It was never conquered, but Habsburg troops blew it up for its part in the 1703–11 War of Independence. The small entrance fee to the castle is worth it for the view from the battlements.

Tapolca

The walk does not pass through this town, but buses serving the Káli-medence villages end up here at some stage. There is a picturesque old water mill and a lake that never freezes in winter. Tapolca is a Slavic word meaning 'warm water', and the ancient Slavs were well aware of the lake's thermal properties. The system of limestone caves beneath the town is popular with sufferers of respiratory illnesses.

Tarányi-Lengyel Wine Press House

One last word from Richard Bright: 'No picture could be more splendidly gay than that part of the landscape which intervened between us and the water'. The doctor was inspired to write this as he stood on the balcony of this eighteenth-century wine press house. There were many built in the Balaton area, and as wine producers spent more time in the vineyards the houses were improved so that they could stay there throughout summer and autumn.

WALK 22
Kuruc-körút

Route:	Badacsony – Szegedi Róza-ház – Rodostó-ház – Szegedi Róza-ház – Badacsony
Distance:	7km (4.5 miles)
Map:	41 Balaton 1:40 000
Transport:	Trains direct to Badacsony from Budapest Déli. If travelling by car cut out the first stage and park at the paying car park above Szegedi Róza-ház museum.
Refreshments:	There are snack bars and pubs around Badacsony railway station or try the more peaceful restaurant and wine bar near the Szegedi Róza-ház museum.

This short circular walk follows a well-waymarked route along hard-packed trails through woodland and around the old basalt quarries. The route was set up in 1953 to commemorate the 250th anniversary of the 1703–11 War of Independence. 'Kuruc' was the name given to the Hungarian rebels who fought a guerrilla war against the Austrians. The origin of the name is unclear but it may refer to the crusader armies of previous times. There are many points along the walk offering good views across the plain to the hills of Szt.György-hegy and sugar loaf Gulács. Training shoes are suitable in summer but some sections of the trail have loose stones. There is plenty of time at the end of the walk to visit the Szegedi Róza-ház museum or relax at the adjacent wine bar.

Look around the crowded snack bars at the back of Badacsony railway station for the waymarks guiding the route up towards Badacsony Hill. Otherwise, to avoid the crowds, start at the station offices and turn left along the platform and then left again to cross

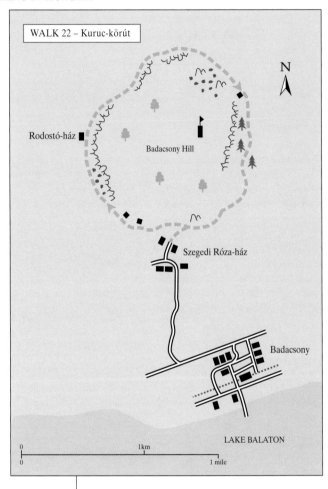

WALK 22 – Kuruc-körút

N

Rodostó-ház

Badacsony Hill

Szegedi Róza-ház

Badacsony

LAKE BALATON

0		1km	
0			1 mile

the little park to a street. Head straight up the street between a restaurant and a tourist office. At the T-junction turn left to follow the road. Turn right on a long asphalt road ascending Badacsony's lower slope. After the road swings left passing some houses take the next right for the **Szegedi Róza-ház** museum. After the museum and a wine bar the road ends at a car park.

To continue up the hill follow the rocky causeway on the left. At its end there is a picnic site with an information board; turn left to pick up a red-waymarked path into the woods. The trees soon give way to reveal a field and a view of **Lake Balaton**. From here the footpath becomes a single-lane asphalt road and passes houses and another information board explaining the region's viniculture. Boulder fields and cliffs rise up to the right. Eventually the red waymarks indicate a path on the right. Follow it uphill through woodland to pass some basalt pillars and boulder fields. The narrow path skirts the back of the thatched **Rodostó-ház** and joins an access road. A few paces later turn right on a footpath entering the forest.

The path zigzags up the wooded slope to a clearing with an old basalt quarry and another information board. There are good views from here. Pick up the red waymarks to continue contouring the hill to the crossroads of red- and blue-waymarked routes. The path ascending right leads to the rock formations of Kő-kapu (Stone Gate) but keep straight ahead on the red waymarks. Ignore the next turn-off for the red (circle) route and pass an old hut. The trail passes another quarry with an information board. Take a left for a path traversing down a steep slope. There is some loose rock but the path levels out passing through bushes, scrub and eventually pine woods. Take the next track right. Continue to descend. The path narrows here and contours the hill and eventually closes the circle by descending the rough flag-stoned path down to the picnic area.

WALK 23
Badacsony to Szigliget

Route:	Badacsony – Korkovány – Gulács – Kisapáti – Szt.György-hegy – Szigliget
Distance:	20.5km (12.5 miles)
Map:	41 Balaton 1:40 000
Transport:	To return, local buses connect Szigliget with Badacsony railway station.
Refreshments:	Plenty of villages *en route*

This long walk around Balaton's volcanic remnant hills offers splendid views of Lake Balaton. Most of the route is well waymarked, which is just as well as many of the tracks passing through vineyards and around the back of holiday houses are not clear on the map. Training shoes and shorts are fine, but there is some loose rock on the descent through Kő-kapu and a section is overgrown. Part of the walk unavoidably follows minor roads although there is little traffic until the busy Highway 71. The basalt columns on Szt.György-hegy are an easy scramble, but can be avoided by taking another route to the right of the steps in front of the hostel.

For the first section start at Badacsony railway station and follow the beginning of the Kuruc-körút in Walk 22 to the picnic site and information board above **Szegedi Róza-ház** museum. At the picnic site turn right on the red-waymarked path and turn left to climb the steps marked by the red (triangle). At a monument bear around to the left and continue to climb the steps, although a little diversion on the right will give a panoramic view of Lake Balaton. Continue uphill but turn right for a rocky footpath and join the blue-way-marked route rising gently to a stone shelter and picnic

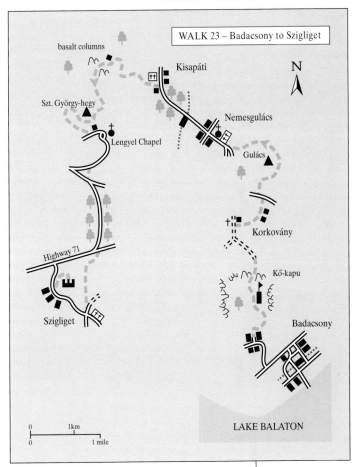

WALK 23 – Badacsony to Szigliget

basalt columns
Kisapáti
Szt. György-hegy
Nemesgulács
Lengyel Chapel
Gulács
Korkovány
Highway 71
Kő-kapu
Szigliget
Badacsony

N

0   1km
0   1 mile

LAKE BALATON

area. Take a sharp right ignoring the Blue Route turn-off for now, and continue to the observation tower for good views of Szt.György-hegy and Gulács.

To continue on the walk, backtrack from the tower and turn right for the blue-waymarked trail passed earlier. As it descends the steep hill, look for a narrow cutting going off to the right. Waymarking is good from here and there is no doubt about the route – the narrowing path with loose rock descends between the columns of Kő-kapu and piles of scree giving glimpses of Gulács. At the fork below the rocks turn left down to a crossroads of blue- and red-waymarked trails. Follow the Blue Route down to a gravel road. After passing vineyards and houses the road swings left giving a good view of Gulács. Leave the road on the slightly overgrown rough track dropping right past the vineyards of **Korkovány**. Turn right to join an asphalt road; it descends to a little round-about with a roadside cross and telephone kiosk. Take a right turn for a road passing an old church hall and bell tower. After the cemetery leave the road on a narrow path down to the left; it rises through a cut-ting and climbs up onto vineyards. The wider track veers left past a line of little houses and joins a main road. Turn left to follow the road for a few paces and turn right at the first track. After a wine cellar the track begins to climb the lower slope of Gulács.

The track turns sharply right passing some houses and from here there are views of the stone pillars of Kő-kapu. At its end the track enters the forest and becomes a rough trail ending at a fork. Turn left for a narrow path ascending through the forest. After swinging right to contour the hill there is a junction of waymarks. Take the green trail rising left but ignore the blue (triangle) path to the summit of Gulács. Follow the green waymarks closely as the path descends to a good track and enters denser forest. The route eventually exits. Approach the fence straight ahead and turn right on the track passing stables and a cemetery before coming into Nemesgulács.

Cross over Nemesgulács main street and con-tinue straight ahead to follow the opposite street leading downhill. Cross the railway line and follow the tree-lined road to the next village, Kisapáti. Pass the little square and park on the right, but after the next park with a war memorial turn left. After the cemetery there is a junction of three tracks: take the middle route, and from here the stony road climbs through the vineyards of Szt.György-hegy. At the T-junction turn right, passing a wine cellar, after which it becomes a little rocky track swinging right past small vineyards and summer houses. After the last house the track narrows to a footpath, passing through woods to a large fenced field with a house. Follow the path along the fence to the roughly surfaced road and turn left up past more houses. At the red sign *Turistaház 300m* turn right as indicated along the narrow-walled footpath through a vineyard and into woodland. At the rough forest track with green waymarks, turn left and follow it uphill to the old *Turistaház* with picnic tables.

Opposite the building there are little steps heading up through the woods. Follow them to the rocky blue-waymarked trail. The gradient increases and the trail disappears on the approach to the **basalt columns**. It is an easy scramble up through the columns and at the top the footpath takes over again.

Szt.György-hegy

For the summit of Szt.György-hegy continue straight ahead on the track passing through a little valley of mixed scrub and pine trees. Waymarking is poor, but after passing a ruined rain shelter the path leaves the last clump of bushes behind and the double bumps of the summit of Szt.György-hegy become visible. Head for the highest point on the right (with the bench) for stunning views of **Lake Balaton**.

To descend, turn away from Lake Balaton and pick up the trail heading straight for the woods. Follow the red-waymarked path turning left through the pine trees and eventually traversing down across areas of open scrub. Turn left at the forest track, but at the *cul de sac* roadsign turn right for the track descending through oak woods. Join a gravel road left. The road surface gradually improves and after houses begins to veer right, but continue straight ahead on a rough track with a field on the left. At a cottage veer right to join a road. At the next road turn left. According to the map the official route turns right after a few yards to descend through the vineyards, but the waymarks have disappeared and there is no obvious path. To avoid trampling over private land, continue straight ahead on the asphalt road passing the **Tarányi-Lengyel Wine Press House**. Cross straight over the roundabout for the **Lengyel Chapel** and turn right to follow the good road downhill.

After some time the road veers right. Look for the waymarks indicating a barely discernible path down across the rough ground on the left. The overgrown track becomes more distinct as it passes through vineyards and eventually joins the main road. Turn left to follow the long straight road lined with trees to busy Highway 71. Take care when crossing the busy highway and pick up a track on the other side. After veering away from the noisy highway and passing vegetable plots the track joins a narrow asphalt access road. At the quiet main road turn right and follow the road up to **Szigliget**. At the little roundabout continue straight ahead for the castle.

WALK 24
Gyulakeszi to Köveskál

Route:	Gyulakeszi – Csobánc – Mindszentkálla – Szentbékkálla – Fekete-hegy – Köveskál
Distance:	16km (10 miles)
Map:	41 Balaton 1:40 000
Transport:	Buses between Révfülöp on Lake Balaton and Tapolca stop at Gyulakeszi. At Köveskál, the end of the walk, catch a bus back to Tapolca or on to Révfülöp with rail links back to Budapest.
Refreshments:	Villages on the way have one or two places to buy refreshments.

The walk meanders on good trails up and down vineyard-covered hillsides. Csobánc and Fekete-hegy give panoramic views down to the Káli-medence and Lake Balaton. On the approach to Mindszentkálla note that Cartographia's map (unless it has been revised) shows the National Blue Route following the vineyard road left; this section of the route is now closed. Ignore the map and follow the revised route into Mindszentkálla. It is possible to do this route as a day walk from Budapest, but start early.

Leave Gyulakeszi by taking the broken road past the church and across rough pasture towards Csobánc hill looming up ahead. At the three-way split follow the middle track for the green route. Take the next left where the track goes through a cutting heading for the vineyards. At the junction with a roadside cross turn left, then right, picking up the green waymarks painted on the stone dyke. After the Rossztemplom, a church which was left to decline after the population fled from the Ottomans, take the track with green (L) waymarks on the right and follow it to the meadow

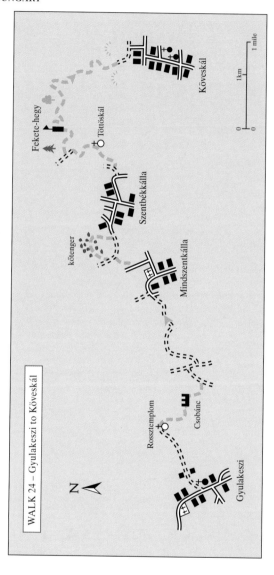

WALK 24 – Gyulakeszi to Köveskál

Fekete-hegy

on the summit of **Csobánc**. Gain the castle ruin for the best view of the day of **Lake Balaton** and the surrounding plain.

To continue the walk retrace steps back down to the meadow but turn right along a narrow footpath through the long grass. Turn right at the next fork and gain the edge of the slope. Veer right along the edge of the hill to find a steep and rocky path descending through bushes. Where the trees take over blue (L) waymarks appear. Near the bottom join a wider track left, then turn right to pass a house, then left again onto another track. At the fork continue left on the blue-waymarked track descending to a farm road. Turn right and follow the road for a short while before leaving at the next left up a roughly paved road to an old farm building. The road switches left then right around the other side of the farm. The track now climbs over the hill and swings left on the other side, passing cottages and a well. At the T-junction of tracks turn right on the blue-waymarked trail ascending through woodland to the saddle where basalt crags can be seen on the hill over to the right.

Continue straight ahead to cross the meadow, and as the path passes a national park sign it drops through bushes past a small house. Join the good track and turn left, passing through more cottages before swinging right to cut straight through a large vineyard. Approaching the end of the vineyard the track bears right, then left to enter Mindszentkálla village. Follow the road round, passing the cemetery, but take the first left leaving the village. At the bus stop turn left for the Reiterhof Panzió access road. There is no need to walk its whole length; look for the blue-waymarked path leaving right. Follow this track until it comes to a dead end with a *No trespassers* sign (in English). Turn right; the path follows a field to a T-junction. Turn left to follow the good track before coming to a grassy spur with scattered rocks on the right. This is the Szentbékkálla **kőtenger**.

Climb the slope past the information board and at the top veer left to pick up the occasional blue waymark painted on the stones. After a short while the route drops left between some rocks and passes along and below the boulder edge for a while. The path then swings right, crossing the other end of the boulder field, after which it descends to a track to join a rough road. Turn left, and after the stations of the cross the track enters **Szentbékkálla** village.

At the main street turn right and then take the first road left past a thatched public building. The road leaves the village. At the wayside cross the road makes a sharp bend to the right, but continue straight ahead across a little stone bridge. Follow the track along the wall and take the next right, then left, to follow a track uphill past a vineyard. At the next fork the ruined church of Töttöskál can be seen up on the right with an information board in English. After the ruins return to the fork and continue on the route by passing the little white-washed house. Ahead, the track appears to invade the privacy of another house. Continue uphill and veer left to skirt a small vineyard. The route eventually descends and a lot of height is lost. This is frustrating, but once at the bottom head for the narrow cutting flanked with bushes to regain the lost metres. At the top there is a vineyard. Continue straight uphill and keep to the blue waymarks in order to avoid private property. At the top turn left along the asphalt road passing a spring called Öreg-hegyi kút and another wayside cross. As the road contours the hill there are a couple of turns for the holiday cottages above, but the correct right turn is where the road begins to descend. A blue waymark on a telegraph pole confirms the route.

This track ascends for a short while before switching back to contour the hill. After the last house there is a fork. Take the left branch; the rough track enters the woods and veers left and around a cabin. Follow the cutting up through the forest. Do not slog all the way to the top – look for blue waymarks indicating a narrow path leaving right for the remaining ascent to the Eötvös Károly wooden observation tower on the summit of Fekete-hegy.

After the tower the National Blue Route continues on a narrow path along the edge of the hill for a short stretch before turning right and descending the steep wooded hill. At the bottom follow the grassy lane past a house to join a track. Turn left and then take the first right to continue downhill. This is the blue (+) route but the waymarking is confusing. To keep it simple follow the winding progress of the track as it descends through vineyards and vegetable plots to Köveskál village.

THE BUDA HILLS

The residents of Budapest are fortunate to have such a large area of forest and park land within a short tram or bus journey from their front doors. The hills are never far, and the familiar landmark of 527m (1728ft) János-hegy is visible from the city streets. Walks in the Buda Hills are not particularly interesting, but as they are so accessible and visible from Budapest they have been included for completeness. The range is a chain of forested hills with bald meadow tops and limestone out-crops which swings around from north-east of the city to the south-eastern industrial estates, skirting suburbs along the way. The Celts of the Eravisci tribe recognised the strategic potential of the precipices overlooking the Danube and built a fort on Gellért-hegy. Romans, Tartars and Turks have passed through to subjugate, pacify, enslave and tax the population. In February 1945 up to 3000 German soldiers breaking out from the siege of Budapest retreated through the wooded hills to avoid Soviet armour. Today, there are only regiments of smart villas marching up the valleys. Although the red roofs of the rich suburbs of Rózsadomb look pictur-esque from a distance the unrestricted development has blighted much of the eastern slopes, with adverse conse-quences for wildlife.

Children's railway

Visitors with children might consider hopping on the *Gyermekvasút* (children's railway). This charming relic is one aspect of Communism not consigned to the dust-bin of history in 1989. Opened in 1948, its construction was a joint venture of the Communist youth movement called the Úttörők (Pioneers) and the Hungarian State Railway. Boys and girls between the ages of 10 and 14 continue to run the railway, but recruits are no longer exclusively from the Pioneer movement, which is no longer a state organisation. Only children with the highest school marks are accepted as volunteers, and successful applicants attend a four-month training course. The average working day starts about 7am. There are eight little stations along the 11km (6.5 miles) of the line and the delightful journey through the forest takes about 50 minutes. At the northern terminus there is a museum about the railway's history but, more importantly, a snack bar selling coffee, snacks, ice cream and beer. The train terminates at Hűvösvölgy, from where regular trams and buses depart for the centre of Budapest.

Routes

With Budapest's two million inhabitants literally a stone's throw away there is a lot of pressure on the Buda Hills, therefore the routes need no more than a brief mention. The walking is not spectacular, the hills are built up in places and the main road is never far away, but it offers a quick escape from noisy Budapest. There is an opportunity to avoid the crowds on some of the less popular woodland trails. The walking chugs along at 400–500m (1300–1650ft) above sea level and there are good views from its hilltop observation towers. There are plenty of opportunities for refreshments on the way.

Cartographia's Map 6 (A Budai-hegység 1:30 000) is invaluable for following the large network of way-marked trails. Three routes actually start in the city, but avoid this tedious walk-in through the suburbs by catching the Metro to Moszkva tér, from where there are buses or trams to the top. An alternative is the funicular train (*Fogaskerekű vasút*) from Városmajor terminus, after which the route has to pass suburban gardens and follow a main road before it begins to look anything like a hill walk. There are many way-marked trails following the long chain of hills, but the route north between the central range and the village of Solymár is the best walk. For fewer buildings and less traffic there is also a circular walk around the forests of the Fekete-hegyek to the west or the grassy tops of Nagyszénás: take the number 63 bus from Moszkva tér to the village of Nagykovácsi to pick up the waymarks.

THE MECSEK

Its position west of the Danube places the Mecsek in Transdanubia, but it is quite distinct from the other ranges of the region. Lying almost 140km (90 miles) south of Budapest, the Mecsek is physically separated by quite a distance from the Transdanubian highlands. Its limestone, sandstone and coal deposits were formed during the Permian and Triassic periods, but there are also granite relics of the European mountain system which was raised over 300 million years ago. Karstic action has created caves and sinkholes around the western hills, but the landscape

Walkers' Memorial, Dobogó, Mecsek

mainly comprises deep forested valleys cut by vigorous streams, broad wooded spurs and, in the west, a steep escarpment. The range has rather low mountains: Zengő, in the eastern part of the range, is the

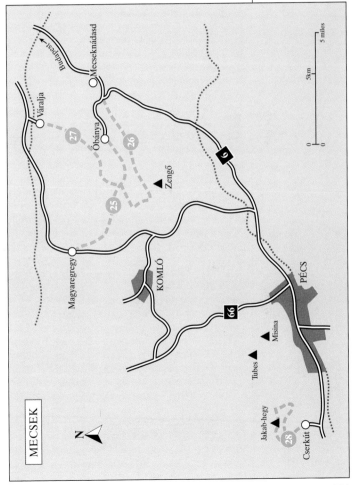

highest summit at 682m (2237ft); and 535m (1755ft) Misina and 611m (2004ft) Tubes provide a backdrop to the city of Pécs.

History

Permanent settlement began about 6000 BC, and between 1000 and 400 BC the Illyrians migrated north from the Balkans and built the earth forts and burial mounds we can see today on Jakab-hegy. Celts migrating south captured the region, but around 400 BC the Roman Empire annexed the area west of the Danube and the Mecsek became part of Pannonia. Huns, Goths and Longobards followed on the heels of the departing Romans but left few structures to remind us of their importance. The Avars came later but were eventually eclipsed by the eastward expansion of the Franks. By the tenth century the Magyars dominated the region until the Turks annexed it for the Ottoman Empire. In the early eighteenth century the Habsburgs brought in German settlers to work the glass foundries, and today many people in the Mecsek define themselves as Swabians. During the 1956 Revolution the conflict in Pécs and Komló spilled over into the hills where the Mecsek Invisibles, a rebel unit comprising miners, army mutineers and students, fought a guerrilla war against Soviet armour and Hungarian police units.

Hungary has been exploiting the extensive coal deposits of the Mecsek since the 1890s, and by the 1950s Komló had expanded to become a mining town. Mining technology was quite advanced during the Communist period and as a result of the push for coal the miners were considered a privileged group. By the 1960s Hungarian technology had fallen behind. When coal fields in the north of Hungary were closed many miners were redeployed to the Mecsek or ended up working in the uranium mines. The last pit was closed in 1999 with dire consequences for Komló's 30 000 inhabitants.

Routes

From the walker's point of view, the range can be divided into two areas: the east and the rest. Mining has disfigured the hills around Komló and the southern valleys above Pécs. In the west deserted mine shafts (*akna*) tower eerily above a sea of forest. With the exception of the short climb up the western escarpment of Jakab-hegy, the best walking is in the Keleti-Mecsek (East Mecsek), which avoided the worst of the twentieth-century hunger for minerals. The walking follows deep valleys and long spurs covered in beech and oak, and passes through small villages. Waymarking is generally quite good.

Transport

There are trains (from Budapest Déli) and buses (from Budapest Népliget) to the city of Pécs, the regional centre for the Mecsek. From Pécs bus station there are many bus services to the walk-in points. One bus a day goes direct from Budapest to Mecseknádasd, the best access point for the eastern valleys.

Accommodation

A free brochure listing a selection of local accommodation is available from Pécs Tourinform. Small hotels, guesthouses and private rooms can be found in most villages. Note that the hostel in Óbányai-völgy is now closed.

Points of interest in the Mecsek

Avar-gyűrű

Set on the summit of Jakab-hegy, this is the largest earth fort in Europe. Its name suggests a connection with the Avars, but the first occupants were Illyrians who were later deposed by Celts. Seven hundred grave mounds were found nearby; follow the blue waymarks west of the ramparts to view some examples.

Babás-szerkövek

Literally Doll Stones, there is a legend about the outcrops. Two feuding families who lived below Jakab-hegy refused alms to a passing beggar and beat him for his impudence. The beggar cursed them. One day both families faced each other on the narrowest part of the trail up to the monastery. Neither side would give way and declared that they would rather be turned to stone and the beggar's curse obliged.

Cserkút

Longobard graves with silver jewellery were unearthed in the village. This people of Scandinavian origin had migrated south and reached Pannonia as the last of the Romans departed. Their tenure was short (about 40 years). They agreed to leave the land to their allies, the Avars. In AD 568 they ended up in northern Italy, where they founded the kingdom of Lombardy.

Gergely-Éva-forrás

Gergely and Éva were two leading characters in the historical novel *Egri csillagok* (*The Heroes of Eger*) by Géza Gárdonyi. Although the climax of the novel is the Ottoman siege of Eger Castle in northern Hungary, the story begins at nearby Máré Castle.

Glass foundries

Glass-making in the Mecsek dates back to the eighteenth century, and the task of maintaining and guarding the kilns set deep in the forests was given to young single men called *hamus legény* (ash lads). They supplemented their income by robbing travellers, earning them the alternative sobriquet *hamus betyár* (ash highwaymen).

Jakab-hegy monastery

Founded in 1225 and devoted to Saint Jakab, the ruins were the focal point of the Hungarian Paulian order named after Saint Paul of Thebes. Banditry in the region forced the monks to abandon the area and many of its stones were sold afterwards. This summit is a potentially pleasant spot, but the elaborate shelter and tower, picnic site, litter and the use of the ruin's stones as fireplaces have degraded the site.

Kisújbánya

In the eighteenth century German settlers worked in quarries nearby to extract silica for the local glass foundries. When the demand for glass declined they became stockbreeders and herders and founded this village, giving it the name Little New Mine.

Depopulation, partly as a result of the centralising policies of Communism, has transformed the village into a neat and rather soulless little place full of holiday homes.

Kővágószőlős

This is an old settlement and has a thirteenth-century church. Its name is created from the three words 'stone', 'woodcutter' and 'vintner', representing the traditional trades of the village. For a history of the village's less traditional occupation visit the uranium mine exhibition.

Magyaregregy

This German minority village was set up as a market town in the Middle Ages. Its Mária chapel is a pilgrimage site.

Máré-vár

Built in 1316 in Gothic style, the castle was converted into a palace in 1530 and is one of Hungary's remaining Renaissance structures. In 1543 Ottoman troops occupied the fort in order to guard the trade route. An accidental explosion in the gunpowder store almost destroyed the building. Tradition has it that a gypsy captain used the castle as a base for his bandit operations, earning it the nickname 'robber fort'. It now houses an excellent little museum with exhibits of the flora and fauna of the East Mecsek and is open from mid-April to mid-October.

Óbányai-völgy

The nature reserve in this valley exists largely through the efforts of Dr Endre Peceli who, with the help of his family, cleared the trail, built the wooden bridge, cleaned the stream and campaigned to keep the area free from development. The monument along the trail was erected in his memory.

Óbánya

Formerly Altglashütte, a few inhabitants can trace their origins to the original settlers from the Black Forest. Today, villagers have held on to their German dialect, and the names of the surrounding hills (Langehöhe, Kólenplatten, Kappenvasszer) are evidence of the influence of these eighteenth-century settlers who came to work the glass foundries. It was once an important centre for pottery and many villagers carry on the tradition.

Püspökszentlászló

Set picturesquely in a valley deep in the hills, this settlement was originally the summer residence of the Bishop (Püspök) of Pécs. The manor house, built in 1797, and its arboretum are closed to the general public. The second half of its name comes from the local legend that Szent László (Saint Ladislas) was on a hunting trip in the area and sheltered in a nearby cave during a violent storm.

Réka-vár

The remains of the fort are now overgrown by trees, but the extensive earthworks and stone wall visible on the north side give the impression that it was once a major fortification. Its foundations might date back to the Romans or Eastern Franks, but there is also a tradition that Attila the Hun built it for his wife Réka.

Skóciai Szent Margit

This cross commemorates Saint Margaret of Scotland whose father, Edward, son of Edmund Ironside, had come to the Hungarian court as a refugee after the Danish Conquest. Margaret was born in Réka-vár, the ruins of which lie on the hill above, but returned to England as a child. When she became the wife of Malcolm III, King of Scotland, she introduced the popular name Alexander. It has been said that her experiences in recently converted Hungary left a mark on this devout Scottish queen who set about trying to reform the Scottish church. A corner of the Mecseknádasd Catholic church is devoted to her.

Váralja

Váralja means The Foot of the Castle, and remains of an old fort can be seen on the hill to the east of the village. Although it has some accommodation and museums, Váralja is not a tourist village and has traditionally depended on mining. The population includes a large number of Roma as well as people of German origin. There are two museums: the first, a mining museum, is passed on the way in from Farkas-árok; and the second is near the centre on the main street.

Zsongor-kő

This excellent viewpoint is named after a knight called Zsongor who, legend has it, jumped off the rock with his lover to flee the pursuing Turks.

WALK 25
Magyaregregy to Óbánya

Route:	Magyaregregy – Máré-vár – Kisújbánya – Óbánya
Distance:	13.5km (8.5 miles)
Map:	15 Mecsek 1: 40 000
Transport:	Frequent buses between Magyaregregy and Pécs, but limited services between Óbánya and Mecseknádasd
Refreshments:	There is a shop at Magyaregregy to stock up and a bar/restaurant at the turn-off to Máré-vár. The little shop at Kisújbánya has limited opening hours, but there are more facilities in Óbánya.

This gentle walk through the East Mecsek follows part of the Rockenbauer Kék Túra, a section of the National Blue Route named after the maker of the 1980s documentary *One Million Steps Around Hungary*. The forest tracks are easy enough and pass over broad hills and through valleys, but are often very rutted and muddy. The route links the forest villages in easy stages. The minor highway between Magyaregregy and the turn-off for Máré-vár is a 10 minute inconvenience.

Start at the centre of **Magyaregregy** at the bus stop in front of the municipal building. Take the main street south to exit the village and follow the main road. Turn left at Máré-csárda bar and restaurant. The road passes a car park and information board. After a house turn right to cross a bridge. On the other side follow the path uphill through the woods on the red waymarks. The path soon begins to contour left around the little spurs of the hill. Less than half an hour later the path approaches **Máré-vár** castle and picnic site. Continue to contour the remaining spurs, passing a spring called **Gergely-Éva-forrás**. There is

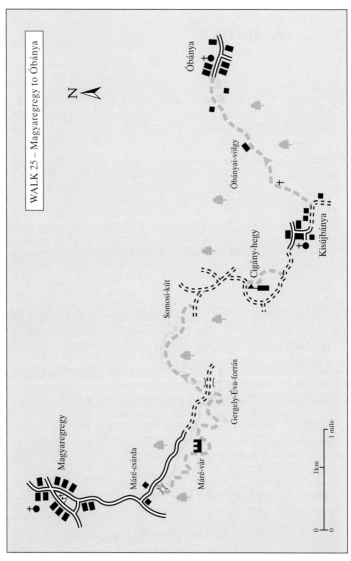

WALK 25 – Magyaregregy to Óbánya

N

Magyaregregy

Máré-csárda

Máré-vár

Gergely-Éva-forrás

Somosi-kút

Cigány-hegy

Kisújbánya

Óbányai-völgy

Óbánya

0   1km

0   1 mile

one last spur before the path descends to cross a rickety bridge and joins the road.

When the road approaches a bridge, drop down to the left for the stream bank. Pick up the red (+) waymarks for a trail which crosses the stream to traverse steeply up the right side of a valley. At a spring called Somosi-kút there is a junction: take the steep yellow-(+)-waymarked track to another junction of rutted tracks. Keep left and then join another forest track with yellow and green (triangle) waymarks. Turn right at the wide forest track and descend to a large junction and clearing. ▶

If there are no waymarks continue to Kisújbánya by taking the second forest track going downhill to the right. At the bottom the track begins to swing right but head up the grassy path to the top of Cigány-hegy. The observation tower is on the right, but veer left on the yellow and green waymark signs to descend to a country road. Turn left for **Kisújbánya**. After the village pump and telephone

Alternative Route
From this junction convert the walk into a short circular route by taking the red-waymarked track to the right and descend to the Máré-csárda road.

Máré-vár

box turn right along a gravel road and at its end turn left to follow the little road flanked by a stream and some houses. When the road swings right turn left to cross the stream and follow the blue and green waymarks to descend a deep valley called **Óbányai-völgy**. After passing an old walkers' hostel, holiday cottages and fish ponds the trail enters **Óbánya**.

WALK 26
Óbánya Circuit (via Réka-vár)

Route:	Óbánya – Réka-vár – Langehöhe – Püspökszentlászló – Kisújbánya – Óbánya
Distance:	18.5km (11.5 miles)
Map:	15 Mecsek 1:40 000
Transport:	Limited buses between Óbánya and Mecseknádasd
Refreshments:	The little shop at Kisújbánya has limited opening hours, but there are more facilities in Óbánya.

This circular route soon leaves the asphalt road to climb up the long and broad spur of Langehöhe and Kólenplatten. The ruins of Réka-vár and some old glass kilns provide historical interest. The walk also passes through the Óbányai-völgy and Hidasi-völgy nature reserves. The going is easy and waymarking good, but during prolonged wet weather the path along Hidasi-völgy can quickly get water-logged and the stream impassable.

Start at **Óbánya** and leave the village on the road to Mecseknádasd, passing the Bambi campsite on the way. Turn right up the slip road with the **Skóciai Szent Margit** wayside cross. There are weekend chalets ahead but pick up the green waymarks to climb the steep wooded spur on the right. At the top the path comes to the earthworks and scattered stones of **Réka-vár**.

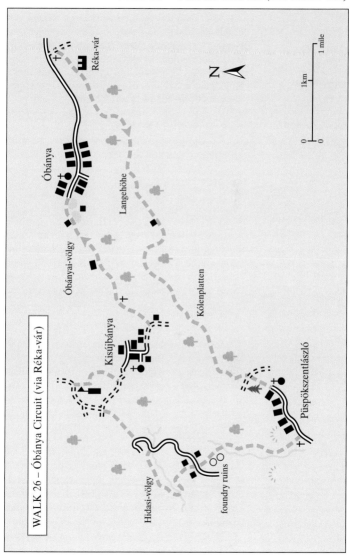

WALK 26 – Óbánya Circuit (via Réka-vár)

Réka-vár

Óbánya

Langehöhe

Óbányai-völgy

Kőlenplatten

Kisújbánya

Püspökszentlászló

Hidasi-völgy

foundry ruins

N

1 mile

1km

0

0

After the ruins continue to follow the track as it undulates along the broad Langehöhe ridge to a clearing and a hunting lodge. There is a crossroads of tracks but continue straight ahead on the green-way-marked track. The route gradually veers around the Kólenplatten chain of little hills. The track approaches the hill of Hárs-tető and the green way-marks deviate from the main trail by following a track descending right. There seems no obvious reason for this diversion, but as this is a strictly protected area follow it round as directed. The yellow-way-marked trail is joined, and after turning left it descends through a gully of pine trees. After crossing a track the trail comes to the back of **Püspökszentlászló**. Turn right to follow the path along the church fence. At the Bazsarózsa *kulcsosház* (cottage) follow the road as it veers left and passes the length of the village. After the last house turn right at the wayside cross into the meadow and descend the track veering right until the bottom. After the waterworks follow the path entering the woods. It follows a fence for a while along the stream. At the end of the trail turn left at the rutted track which crosses the stream. After a while the old **glass foundries** are passed. Continue straight ahead to cross an asphalt forest road to a grassy area with a hunting chalet and picnic tables. Head for the trees to pick up a green-(+)-waymarked path.

Follow the meandering path down the steep hill to the bottom of Hidasi-völgy and find a place to cross the stream. On the other side turn right and follow the blue waymarks along the stream. At the asphalt forest road turn left, but after it bends look for the continuation of the blue-waymarked trail dropping away to the right. From here the trail follows the stream for a while and climbs around the little valley to a rough road. Turn right for **Kisújbánya**.

After the village pump and telephone box turn right along a gravel road and at the end turn left on

*St Margaret of
Scotland cross,
Réka-vár*

a little road flanked by a stream and some houses. After a while the road swings right, but turn left to cross the stream and follow the blue and green waymarks down into **Óbányai-völgy**. After passing an old walkers' hostel, holiday cottages and fish ponds the trail enters **Óbánya**.

WALK 27
Kisújbánya to Váralja

Route:	Kisújbánya – Cigány-hegy – Farkas-árok – Váralja
Distance:	10.5km (6.5 miles)
Map:	15 Mecsek 1:40 000
Transport:	At the end of this walk it is a 45 minute walk from the start of Váralja village to its railway halt, but only slow trains for Dombóvár and Pécs stop here. The timetable is posted on the door of the railway house. There are also buses to Pécs from the bus stop across the road.
Refreshments:	None until Váralja

Although the walk starts in Kisújbánya there is no public transport to the village. It is best treated as an extension of the other routes connecting Óbánya (Walks 25 and 26). The long-deserted Farkas-árok (Wolf's Gully) and its vigorous burn is well way-marked for the most part. Spring thaws and heavy rain can flood sections of the path, and at the lower end of the valley, stream and track merge.

To leave **Kisújbánya** take the road west passing the water pump. Follow the rough road until the turn-off right for the path up to Cigány-hegy. At the top of the hill find the grassy path descending the other side. At the bottom it is joined by a rutted track coming from the left and continues uphill to a cleared area. Waymarks, if there are any, are confusing at the clearing, but turn left and then veer right for the blue (+) waymarks marking a rough forest vehicle track contouring a hill. Do not follow it too far, but pick up a barely noticeable and overgrown lesser trail dropping to the right. It is unmarked, but this is the continuation of the blue (+) route which traverses down the left side of the valley called Farkas-árok. After

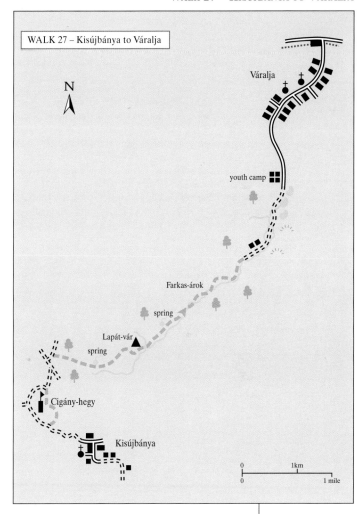

WALK 27 – Kisújbánya to Váralja

N

Váralja

youth camp

Farkas-árok

spring

Lapát-vár

spring

Cigány-hegy

Kisújbánya

0   1km

0   1 mile

the spring marked Lendület-forrás on the map the
path traverses left to climb over the spur. Follow the
top for a while before descending to a saddle. The

hill of Lapát-vár appears straight ahead, but veer right and descend the track into a cutting to meet the stream.

About 10 minutes later the path crosses the Farkas-patak, a tributary of the Váralja burn. There is a turn-off with green (circle) waymarks, but continue straight ahead on the blue (+) waymarks, passing another spring, Kalán Miska kútja. This pleasant section of the route gently descends in a traverse down to the mouth of the valley, where the path broadens to a track and the stream braids as it passes a sand bank. After an animal feeder and some houses the road, now with gravel surfacing, fords the stream a couple of times to pass through park land with a string of fishing ponds and a picnic shelter. After the youth camp the surfaced road continues to the first houses of **Váralja**.

Spring in the forest, Dobogó

WALK 28
Jakab-hegy

Route:	Cserkút – Kővágószőlős – Jakab-hegy – Kővágószőlős
Distance:	10km (6 miles)
Map:	15 Mecsek 1:40 000
Transport:	Local buses between Cserkút, Kővágószőlős and Pécs
Refreshments:	Shops and bars in Cserkút and Kővágószőlős. Do not drink water from the pump on the summit of Jakab-hegy (marked Cigány-kút on the map).

The only walk at the western end of the Mecsek worth considering. The villages of Cserkút and Kővágószőlős are a pleasant start to this short but strenuous climb up the wooded Jakab-hegy escarpment. The hard-packed trails are well marked and the tiny scramble over rocks half-way up is not difficult. Where the trees give way to the stone columns and outcrops of the Babás-szerkövek and Zsongor-kő, there are splendid views of the villages below and across the River Dráva to Croatia.

Starting at the old church in **Cserkút** look opposite for a rough street going uphill. At the top turn left along the village back road. Turn left again for **Kővágószőlős** which is now visible. After passing the old village church and cemetery, leave the village on the next street right rising past household plots. Enter the woods at the national park sign and pick up the steep trail ascending to join the blue-(+)-waymarked route. Follow this waymark until the red (triangle) route. The hard climb eases to a flat contouring walk passing the Jubilee Cross and the **Babás-szerkövek** rock formations. After five minutes leave the red route to rejoin the blue-(+)-waymarked trail which climbs steeply again to the left.

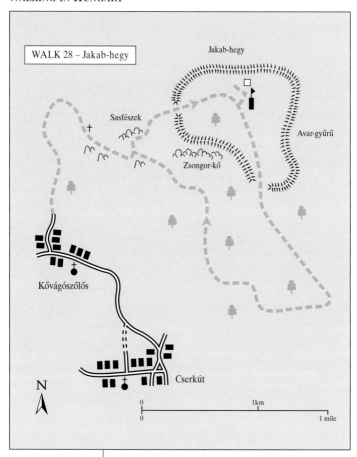

WALK 28 – Jakab-hegy

Jakab-hegy

Sasfészek

Avar-gyűrű

Zsongor-kő

Kővágószőlős

N

Cserkút

0   1km

0   1 mile

Detour
At the old earth ramparts pick up the path descending right to the outcrops of Zsongor-kő for a bird's-eye view.

The trail breaks up here and fallen trees block the way, but try not to lose height. It is another 10 minutes to the Permian sandstone cliff called Sasfészek. Turn sharply right, then left, over an outcrop. There is one last steep section before the top. Take the trail right through a gap in the old earth ramparts of **Avar-gyűrű**. ◀

It is only 10 minutes from here on the blue way-marks to the shelter with its church-like tower and picnic site. To the left of the tower stand the ruins of **Jakab-hegy monastery**. Look around the picnic area for the red route back into the forest. It exits the outer wall and begins to descend a forested spur. At the junction turn right along the red (triangle) route which contours the escarpment until arriving back at the Babás-szerkövek. Retrace the familiar route ascended at the beginning of the walk in order to return to Kővágószőlős.

THE PILIS AND VISEGRÁD HILLS

Between the Buda Hills, the River Danube, the northern suburbs of Budapest and the historic city of Esztergom lie the Pilis and Visegrád Hills. Both ranges are within the Duna-Ipoly National Park, a large protected area which includes the Börzsöny north of the Danube. For route description purposes the two ranges, which share the same map, are treated here as one entity, but from the geologist's point of view they are quite distinct.

The name Pilis is of Slav origin and means 'ton-sure', referring to the many tree-less tops which were

Vadálló-kövek and the Danube, Pilis, Walk 29

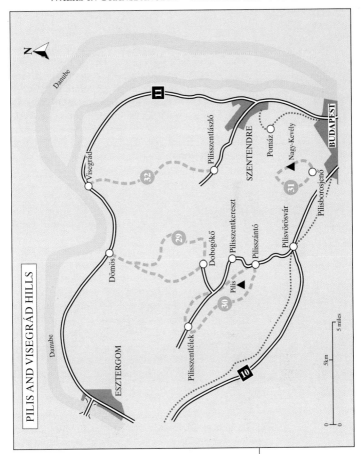

PILIS AND VISEGRÁD HILLS

once a feature of this chain of hills stretching 32km (20 miles) from Budapest's northern suburbs to Esztergom. Its base is dolomite and limestone with an additional layer of sandstone. When tectonic movements shattered the chain, the crags along the western slopes were formed. Today, they are popular with climbers. The highest summit of the Pilis is its eponymous hill at 756m (2480ft), which is also the highest point of the Transdanubian group.

The Visegrád range is placed in the Transdanubian section of this guide, although geologically it belongs to the northern hills, to which it was attached before the Danube separated it from the Börzsöny. The Visegrád's andesite was formed 20 million years ago when it was the centre of massive volcanic activity, which also created the northern highland chain. The hills follow the line of the Danube Bend, giving the range an appearance of a giant croissant. Rolling forested hills and rocky gullies are a common feature in the Visegrád.

History

The Scythians were here and left a few graves with artefacts, but the Celts left more of a mark when they founded Solva (now Esztergom). Commanding the water route down the Danube, Solva became an important centre for the Romans, who renamed it Strigonium (thus Esztergom), deriving from the Greek for Danube, Ister, and the Latin for the River Garam (now the Hron in Slovakia). They also built camps, townships and fortifications along the river, and in the Pilis serious deforestation took place as a result of viticulture. After the legions left in the fourth century AD, waves of Goths, Huns, Avars and Slavs arrived. The Magyars made Esztergom the centre of their power, and later King Béla IV built the great fort of Visegrád to guard the routes along the Danube Bend. During Roman expansionism Marcus Aurelius defeated the Germanic tribes here, but in a more recent conflict their descendants beat a hasty retreat through the forests of the Pilis after breaking out of Soviet-encircled Budapest.

Many villages were abandoned during the Ottoman–Habsburg wars, but after the Turks left Slovaks and Germans settled here and pretty Szentendre still has a thriving Serbian community. Despite the population movements after World War

II. when large numbers of Slovaks and Germans were repatriated, some of their descendants continue to live in the Pilis and have kept their languages and traditions alive.

Routes

Hungary's first walking routes were set up in the Pilis between Dömös and Dobogókő in the nineteenth century and today the hills are as popular as ever. A glance at the map will show that the southern part of the range, the Kevélyek chain, can be approached on foot from Budapest by following the red route from Csillaghegy HÉV. It is a tedious walk-in, however, passing through unattractive new developments or having been obliterated altogether. It is better to catch a bus to the walk-in points and pick up the wonderful little routes following Roman roads and treeless ridges. The going is not difficult, but the route up the Rám-szakadék has fixed chains to aid the ascent in this otherwise dangerous and narrow gorge. On the more popular routes waymarking is quite good, but expect moments of uncertainty as usual. Busy Dobogókő in the centre acts as a bridge between the Pilis and Visegrádi-hegység.

Transport

There are regular bus services from Budapest Árpád híd bus station to both the Pilis and Visegrád ranges. Walk-in points for the Visegrád section are further from the city but still lend themselves to easy day walks. An alternative route to the hills is Budapest's Batthyány tér HÉV line to Pomáz or Szentendre, from where there are local bus services. Allow for up to an hour and a half of travel time if taking public transport to the central range.

Accommodation

If not using Budapest as a base, there are private rooms and hotels in some villages. If looking for a central point then Dobogókő's old MTE hostel, steeped in Hungarian walking history, is the best bet. The quaint Sasfészek walkers' hostel on Fekete-hegy is only available through pre-booking.

Points of interest in the Pilis

Calvary chapel

The chapel built into the rock below the Visegrád fortress was founded in memory of József Viktorin, a priest of Slovakian origin. He was devoted to the exploration of the Visegrád Hills and the conservation of the castle ruins.

Dobogókő

It is hard to imagine that this is a hill summit and is 699m (2293ft) above sea level, although the look-out point behind the hostel gives a better feel for the elevation. A Roman watchtower stood here, but the development today is down to the efforts of the MTE walking club. During the 1950s it was a popular place for distinguished members of the Communist elite to take the air. It was on one such visit that Prime Minister Mátyás Rákosi ordered the destruction of a memorial to walkers who had died in the two wars.

Dömös

For a brief time it looked as if this unlikely little settlement would become the capital of Hungary. Unfortunately the first parliamentary session in 1063 was interrupted when the ceiling fell on King Béla I, who died of his injuries. It was here in 1107 that King Kálmán Könyves made peace with his rebellious younger brother, Prince Álmos, although he blinded him and his son (Béla II) later when he made another bid for the throne. The monastery and church survived the Ottoman years, but Leopold I of Austria had them blown up during the Kuruc uprising in the late seventeenth century.

Egri-vár

Looking down from the crags of Nagy-Kevély the ruined castle below looks real enough, but it is a set constructed for the 1968 film *Egri csillagok* (*The Heroes of Eger*). Directed by Zoltán Várkonyi, the screenplay was based on the 1901 novel by Géza Gárdonyi. In the film the unmistakable backdrop of Nagy-Kevély can be seen behind the fort.

Eötvös Loránd menedékház

Menedékház is Hungarian for 'refuge', and (with the exception of the pre-Trianon Tatras) the wood cabin to its left was the first one in Hungary. The Hungarian Association of Walkers (MTE) built the refuge in 1898. Without belittling their achievements the nineteenth-century pioneers probably did not foresee today's car park, snack bars, tennis courts and the carborne day-trippers who have walked no further than the look-out point behind the hostel. The original cabin is a listed building and museum of MTE history. The stone hostel on the right was built in 1906 and is named after the MTE's first director, the physicist Baron von Eötvös, who is better known for introducing the concept of surface tension and his study of the Earth's gravitational field.

Fekete-hegy (Sas-fészek) hostel

This is one of the many walking hostels built by the MTE walking club and from here the dome of Esztergom's basilica can be seen. The poet József Berda spent a lot of his time walking in the Pilis and the inscription on the plaque quotes him:

> *Our unforgettable Fekete-hegy*
> *In the heart of the Pilis*
> *When can I go up*
> *To you again?*

Kevélynyergi hostel

This unfortunate pile of ruins was a walking hostel built by the working-class walking club the Természetbarátok Turista Egyesülete (Association of the Friends of Nature) in 1928. The hostel took five years to build and several thousand walkers attended its opening. It burnt down in 1991.

Pilisborosjenő

The first recorded settlement, Burusjenew, was founded in 1284 but was destroyed during the Ottoman invasion of 1541. Germans settled in 1691 and called their village Weindorf. They made wine and worked in the stone quarries; the old pits are visible around Aranylyuk on Nagy-Kevély. The monument at the House of Culture is a memorial to the 1270 descendants of the original settlers who were deported to Germany in 1946.

Pilisszántó

The old Roman military road built in the third century AD goes through this Slovakian village.

Pilisszentlászló

There was an ancient settlement here called Kékes, probably founded by the descendants of the tenth-century pagan chieftain Koppány. On the hill where the chapel now stands, there was a hunting lodge. In the thirteenth century King Andrew III gave it to the Hungarian Paulian order to found a monastery. It was destroyed by the Ottomans in 1526 and the village abandoned, but Paulian monks of Slovak origin resettled the area. A chapel, built in 1772, now occupies the hill where the monastery stood. The village was also rebuilt and named Senvaclav, after the Polish-born King Ladislas, but the Hungarian name uses the Magyarised form, László.

Pilisszentlélek

The historical importance of this Slovakian village is attributed to its Paulian monastery. The buildings were destroyed during the Ottoman occupation. Its substantial ruins are situated above the village.

Postás-út

This was a postal route until the end of the eighteenth century. The memorial cross was erected to the memory of a walker.

Prédikálószék

From here the Danube Bend can be seen in all its glory. The outcrop marks the position of the riverbank before the Danube cut the deep gorge we can see today. On the other side the caves visible among the rocks of the Börzsöny hills were hermit cells and continued to be occupied until the early twentieth century. The wooden cross is devoted to Saint Ladislas.

Rám-szakadék

A gully of andesite, its name is an archaic expression meaning 'fall upon me' and pray that the people above you do not. Thank the Pilis Forest Park authorities for the fixed chains.

Redlinger Adolf út

Many tracks, trails and springs were named after important members of Hungary's walking movement. Adolf Redlinger's Way was named after the founding member and chairman of the Természetbarátok Turista Egyesülete (Association of the Friends of Nature) walking club. He was also editor of its journal *Természetbarát Újság*.

Roman road
The Roman road was an important trade and military route linking Strigonium (Esztergom) and the settlements of the Pilis with the important town of Aquincum (now in northern Buda).

Szentfa-kápolna
This place has a long association with miracles, but the Ottomans destroyed the original shrine. The chapel is near the spot where, in 1885, the Virgin and Child appeared to a girl while she was tending geese. The miracle is supposed to reappear on the first full moon of every month. Its name Szentfa (miracle tree) refers to the birch tree where the event took place. There are many miracle trees in the forests of Hungary and they are usually marked on the maps.

Teve-szikla
This exposed section of the Pilis sandstone layer is called Camel Rock because of its shape.

Vadálló-kövek
These outcrops are an eroded section of volcanic agglomerates and have fanciful names such as Attila's Helmet, Árpád's Throne, Monk and Nun, and Cleopatra's Needle. According to legend its name, The Stand of the Game, refers to the era of royal hunts when exhausted deer would rest a while along the ridge only to be picked off by waiting archers. A popular spot for climbers.

Visegrád fortress
From the Slavonic for 'high fort', this impressive stronghold was built as part of King Béla IV's kingdom-wide fortification programme. It took 20 years to build, and during the reign of Róbert Károly (1308–42) became an important centre of Hungarian power. Mátyás (1458–90) made the castle his summer residence. The tradition of this former seat of power in Central Europe continues as the Conference of Visegrád Nations, a forum to discuss regional issues.

WALK 29
Dobogókő Circuit

Route: Dobogókő – Vadálló-kövek – Rám-szakadék – Dobogókő

Distance: 17km (10.5 miles)

Map: 16 Pilis és a Visegrádi-hegység 1:40 000

Transport: Take the Szentendre-bound HÉV railway and get off at Pomáz for buses to Dobogókő. Note that services are limited on weekdays. If taking the quick exit option to Dömös there are buses back to Budapest Árpád híd.

Refreshments: The walk affords time to hang around Dobogókő and perhaps have a meal. There is a good restaurant in the Eötvös Loránd menedékház (refuge), but if finishing early at Dömös on the Danube there is a bar near the bus stop.

This fine circular route has a mixture of forest trails, a dramatic descent on the Vadálló-kövek outcrops with views of the Danube Bend, and an ascent through the Rám-szakadék gorge on fixed chains. The latter requires care as inappropriately shod walkers ignore the one-way rule and insist on descending the gorge. Expect frustrating delays on busy weekends.

Start at **Dobogókő** by facing the stone-built **Eötvös Loránd menedékház** and turn right along the asphalt road. Do not waste time looking for the way-marked route on the map but continue on the road to the gate of the television mast station. Skirt around the right of the fence to pick up a rough track descending through the forest. At a crossroads of waymarked routes take the red-(triangle)-way-marked path left and down the steep hill to an asphalt road. Turn right but take the next rough track leaving left. At the hunters' cottage the track narrows to a footpath and descends a very steep

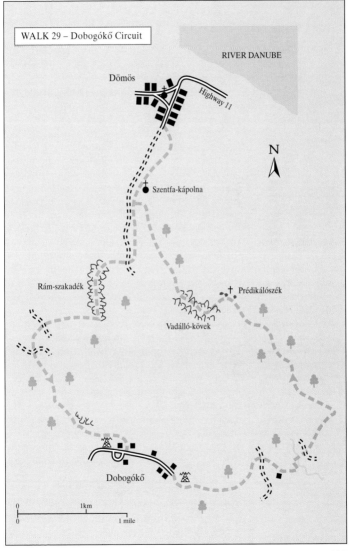

WALK 29 – Dobogókő Circuit

RIVER DANUBE

Dömös

Highway 11

N

Szentfa-kápolna

Rám-szakadék

Prédikálószék

Vadálló-kövek

Dobogókő

0   1km

0   1 mile

slope. Cross the stream at the bottom and climb the bank opposite to a path. Turn right and then sharply left uphill to another forest road. Cross over and pick up the red (triangle) waymarks indicating a footpath going uphill. As the path tops out it joins the red-(+)-waymarked route at a fence.

Turn left along the fence for the red-(triangle)-waymarked track. Ignore any paths joining the track or diverting from it, but look for the fork where the waymarked route leaves the track up to the left. From here the undulating woodland trail climbs a forested spur coming out to the **Prédikálószék** outcrop and wooden cross. Linger a while to take in the grandeur of the Danube Bend before turning away and down to the left to rejoin the red-(triangle)-waymarked trail. The path continues down through the woods to the **Vadálló-kövek** ridge. A narrow path descends the rocky ridge onto a steep wooded spur. ◀

Alternative Route
If the prospect of negotiating slippery Rám-szakadék and its chains is an uninviting one, turn right at the bottom of the wooded spur and follow the trail north along the stream past the Szentfa-kápolna. The track eventually crosses the stream. Turn right and follow the road to Dömös.

Once at the bottom of the wooded spur turn left to pick up the green waymarks. The trail passes through the grounds of an old youth camp and then crosses a stream. At the fork take the right trail with green waymarks. It veers right to cross the road. Continue right to ford another stream. The green waymarks take the path into **Rám-szakadék**.

At the top of the gorge, head straight past the picnic site and reach a road. Cross over and turn left to follow the road for a few paces before turning right up a narrow path through young forest. This is the yellow route, but there are no waymarks and it exits the woods at a forest road. Cross to the other side and pick up the track traversing through scrub. At the top of a spur there is a junction. Turn left to follow the red-waymarked route along a landscaped path and past a television mast. Below to the right are the buildings of Dobogókő. Where the waymarks indicate turn right to pass between the wooden museum and the stone-built hostel to where the walk started.

Negotiating the Rám-szakadék

WALK 30
Pilisszántó Circuit

Route:	Pilisszántó – László kúpja – Fekete-hegyi (Sas-fészek) hostel – Pilisszentlélek – Pilisszántó
Distance:	22km (13.5 miles)
Map:	16 Pilis és a Visegrádi-hegység 1:40 000
Transport:	Regular buses connect Budapest Árpád híd bus station with Pilisszántó. If tempted to stop at Pilisszentlélek and spend the afternoon at the bar, be aware that there are no buses to Budapest and services to Esztergom are limited.
Refreshments:	Conveniently half-way around the walk, charming little Pilisszentlélek has two bars.

A long day out with an easy ascent to the 600m (2000ft) look-out point on the crags of Pilis. Good forest trails, the Slovak village of Pilisszentlélek and a Roman road provide a good combination for this route. The waymarking is good.

If taking the bus do not get off until the terminus at the top of the village of **Pilisszántó**. Dominating the view ahead are the limestone crags of Pilis. Follow the main road out of the village as it ascends towards Pilis. Ignore the first two turnings, but after the road takes a right bend pick up a narrow red-waymarked footpath on the left. Follow it uphill through the woods until a crossroads of tracks and a national park sign. Open country is visible ahead, but turn left on the green waymarks to continue through the trees for a while before the path turns right to exit the woods. The track begins to ascend gently, skirting the woods up the side of Pilis and swinging left back into woodland to contour the hard nose and crags of László kúpja. The map promises a panorama, and the effort is rewarded by an

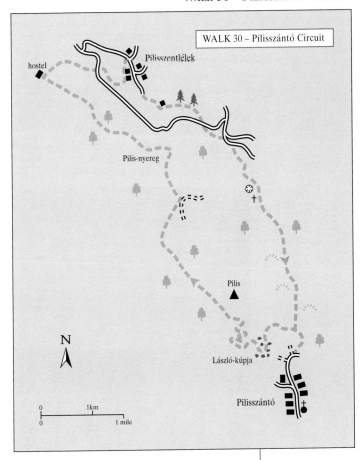

Map: WALK 30 – Pilisszántó Circuit

hostel · Pilisszentlélek · Pilis-nyereg · Pilis · László-kúpja · Pilisszántó

N

0   1km
0   1 mile

excellent view of the Kevélyek chain of hills marching away in the distance.

Continue to follow the trail around the spur.
After switching back and forward several times the
hard stony trail comes to a meadow. Veer left on the
track, passing a hunting tower. After a long straight
contour around the hill the track swings right. Ignore

a misleading continuation of the track ahead but keep left on the green waymarks. From here the track descends to a junction with the red (+) route. Stay on the main track straight ahead, and when it comes to a road veer left and downhill on the green-waymarked track. The contouring resumes and then a junction of trails is reached. Turn left on the narrower joint green/green (+) route down through a steep gully to the picnic site and rain shelter at Pilis-nyereg. The green-waymarked route continues on a wide forest track ascending the next hill to follow the long back of Fekete-hegy. At the waymarked junction join the

Feketehegy hostel

green (square) route right and then left for **Fekete-hegy (Sasfészek) hostel** and a view down the Danube Valley and the dome of Esztergom's basilica.

Leave the hostel on the green (+) footpath traversing down to the right on the steep path called **Postás-út**. There are rough steps cut into the slope and a steel cable attached to trees to aid progress. The path comes to a forest track. Join it and follow it right for a short distance, but look for the continuation of the green (+) route down the left, finishing at a picnic spot. Cross the main road and head for a track re-entering the woods. Craggy Ráró-hegy rises over to the left. After a short walk the green (+) waymarks appear to indicate a continuation through thicker woodland ahead, but take the narrow path left to descend a gully with a stream. At the bottom there is level ground with a little vegetable patch. Veer left to skirt around it and then cross over the stream and climb the bank to a grassy track. Turn right to follow the track down to **Pilisszentlélek**.

At the street there is a bus shelter and village hall. Turn right and follow the length of the village uphill to the end of the street, where a rutted track through a cutting takes over. At the top there is a barrier and on the other side the path is a neat gravelled affair. Pass a works building with a crane and a waterworks. Before the gravel track begins to veer right turn left onto a rough track towards the conifer plantation. The waymarks are missing, but veer right and continue uphill, skirting the wood to its end, where it rises to the main road. Cross the road to pick up a green-waymarked track on the other side and ascend through woodland until rejoining the main road. Follow the road for a few minutes, but ignore the first right turn. Pick up the continuation of the green route re-entering the woods on the right and follow the **Roman road** downhill. Turn left at a junction. Continue past the Ördög-lyuk cave. The wayside cross is a memorial to the death of a local forest engineer. The track passes steep banks, a gully and a cabin, but continue straight ahead on the Roman road until it comes to a junction of tracks with open country ahead. Take the middle route rising slightly to pass a few summer houses and follow it across bushy heath and meadow. This is the yellow (+) route, but there are few trees along the way with waymarks. The hill rising to the right is Pilis. The track re-enters the woods above Pilisszántó bringing the walk full circle. Turn left then right for the red-waymarked trail down to the main road to the village.

WALK 31
Nagy-Kevély

Route:	Pilisborosjenő – Nagy-Kevély – Teve-szikla – Pilisborosjenő
Distance:	6.5km (4 miles)
Map:	16 Pilis és a Visegrádi-hegység 1:40 000
Transport:	Regular buses connecting to Budapest
Refreshments:	Limited, but there is a shop and bar in Pilisborosjenő.

This short circular walk up to the limestone crags of Nagy-Kevély offers a good day out with easy and quick access from Budapest. It is a popular area on weekends so expect to share the day with picnicking families. Note that military exercises, which normally take place at a safe distance west of the gully called Solymári-völgy, can spill over into the meadow and scrub around the ruin of Egri-vár. It is a popular place for walking, but avoid map square 2204 altogether.

Starting at **Pilisborosjenő** go up Templom utca past the church following the red (square) and yellow waymarks. At a T-junction turn right to follow Szent Donát út and take the next left uphill on a rough village street which ends at a pine wood. Enter the forest, turning sharply left along a narrow trail through a cutting to eventually traverse uphill. The path switches back, then swings left to join the red-waymarked track. Turn left, passing the old quarry pits. The red-way-marked path ascends the steep spur to the limestone crags of Nagy-Kevély. There is a good view over to

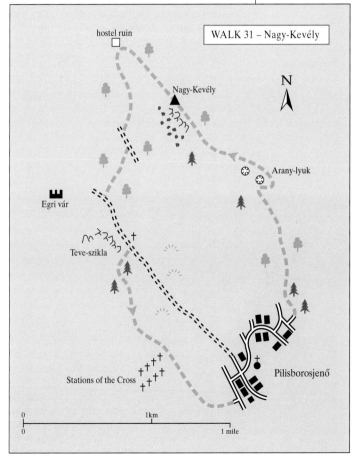

227

the Buda Hills, and in the valley below the walls of **Egri vár** are visible.

Pass the disused look-out tower on the summit and take the path descending the long trail on the other side to a broad wooded saddle. Ahead lies the demolished remains of **Kevélynyergi hostel** and a track junction. Turn left to swing around and down the stony track marked by blue, yellow and green waymarks called **Redlinger Adolf út**. The track descends to a junction with a picnic site. Here the green route leaves to the right, but continue straight ahead on the blue and yellow waymarks. Turn at the next right, where the track splits, and keep to the blue waymarks. The track descends the hill to a T-junction at the bottom. Turn left, still on the blue waymarks. The route comes to open country and from here the limestone rocks on Nagy Kevély are visible up on the left. Straight ahead is the village of Pilisborosjenő, but turn right at the wayside cross to the end of a quarry. To the right the **Teve-szikla** rock

Winter scene,
Nagy-Kevély

formation stands, but turn left to pick up the blue waymarks which continue over a conifer-topped hillock. The grassy path passes through scrub and heath. Cross over the muddy track and pick up the blue waymarks leading the way past the stations of the cross. Follow the straight track as it skirts the back of Pilisborosjenő and drop left on a rough footpath between the houses. Turn left at the street, passing a bar. Cross the little bridge on the right to gain the main street and turn left for the wooden bus shelter in front of the council building.

WALK 32
Szent László Valley and Visegrád Fortress

Route:	Pilisszentlászló – Szent László-völgy – Apát-kúti-völgy – Visegrád fortress
Distance:	12km (7.5 miles)
Map:	16 Pilis és a Visegrádi-hegység 1:40 000
Transport:	Frequent buses connect Visegrád with Budapest and can be caught from one of the bus stops on Highway 11, which follows the Danube bank.
Refreshments:	There is a snack bar at the Visegrád fortress car park, but more facilities can be found in the town of Visegrád.

Pilisszentlászló, situated at the heart of the Visegrád Hills, is the hub of six waymarked trails radiating out from the village, providing numerous day walks. This route passes through the beech forest of the Szent László and Apát-kút valleys. Trails are easy underfoot, with a couple of stream crossings. Apart from the closing stretch leading up to Visegrád fortress there is little gradient to deal with. The fortress is very busy in summer, but the panorama from its battlements high above the Danube Bend is

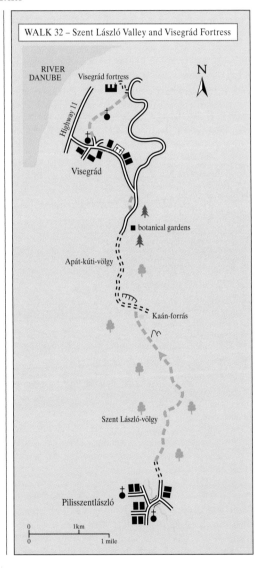

WALK 32 – Szent László Valley and Visegrád Fortress

RIVER DANUBE

Visegrád fortress

N

Highway 11

Visegrád

botanical gardens

Apát-kúti-völgy

Kaán-forrás

Szent László-völgy

Pilisszentlászló

0   1km
0   1 mile

worth the short climb. There is an entrance fee. In the long light evenings of summer it is possible to catch a Danube ferry back to Budapest. Ferries operate from April to October.

From **Pilisszentlászló** bus stop cross the street and veer left then pass the chapel and follow the road over the little bridge over a stream. Turn left for the red waymarks to leave the village. The track follows the valley uphill, and below to the left on the other

Calvary chapel, below Visegrád fortress

side there are summer houses and hunting lodges. The track narrows to a footpath and ascends into mature beech forest, but later joins the stream bank. When the steep embankment requires it the track crosses the stream for better walking. Half-way through the walk, outcrops appear a little up the hill on the right. The path eventually joins a forest road at a rain shelter and picnic site. Follow the road to pass a quarry and hunting lodge. At the Bertényi Miklós Botanical Gardens there is a car park, picnic site and totem pole, and the road improves. The waymarks avoid the asphalt road and tourist traffic to follow the Apát-kúti-patak stream as it leaps over rocks, but sooner, rather than later, the path is compelled to join the road.

Continue along the long road into Visegrád town, and after the cemetery take the next street heading up to the right. Look for a blue waymark on a concrete telegraph pillar to confirm the correct turning. After a few paces take the second turning left. The track narrows to a footpath as it ascends to a picnic site. Continue uphill past stations of the cross. Keep above and to the right of the tiny **Calvary chapel** built into an andesite column. The path soon comes to the car park at **Visegrád fortress**. Descend by retracing steps back down the hill, but turn right at the street for the centre of Visegrád and the Danube.

THE VÉRTES

This oval Triassic block about 50km (30 miles) west of Budapest was part of the Austrian Alps, although every Hungarian landscape type can be found here, perhaps earning it the name Hungary in Miniature. The northern slopes are damp with boggy meadows, and the wooded north–south central ridge is crisscrossed with dry valleys eventually flattening to a plateau. At its southern end there is a dolomite escarpment of Mediterranean karst, but the western slope (Vértesalja) falls away more gently. At the

Vértes Escarpment,
Vértes, Walk 33

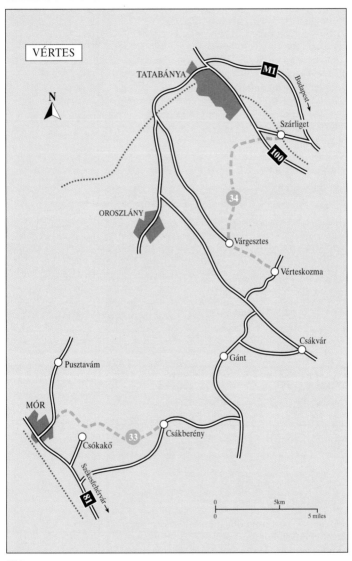

north end of the range lies the mining town of Tatabánya. The wide Mór Valley separates the Vértes from the Bakony range. Most settlements are strung around the hills in a circle at the entry points of valleys, but Várgesztes, Vérteskozma and Kőhányás lie within the north central part of the range.

History

Vért is an archaic word meaning 'armour' and might refer to an unsuccessful invasion by the Holy Roman Empire when routed German troops retreating through the Vértes dropped their shields in their haste. During the sixteenth and seventeenth centuries the disputed border between Habsburg and Ottoman Hungary cut through the Vértes, and its castles, forming a defensive line, changed hands frequently. Centuries of warfare have taken their toll and, with the exception of Várgesztes, the castles are now in ruins. During World War II the range was once more on the frontline; it took the Soviet army only one day to push through the Vértes and within two days it controlled the Mór Valley. The forests were a favourite place for the kings of Hungary, who came here to hunt.

Routes

The range has rather low summits, not rising much higher than 450m (1500ft), but the walking provides a good day out. Start early and set a good pace, and it is possible to complete the 40km (25 mile) route from Szárliget to Mór in a day, but sections of the trail are poorly marked. The two walks below provide the best walking and either start in the north and head for the centre or follow the top of the southern escarpment, which has the best views.

Transport

Public transport from Budapest to the Vértes is efficient and fast. For most walk-in points take a train from Budapest Déli to Szárliget, Tatabánya or Mór.

Buses depart from Budapest Népliget, but it might be necessary to change at Székesfehérvár for local services.

Accommodation
This is a perfect range for day walks from Budapest, but there is accommodation in the villages. For something more unusual try the castle, Gesztesi-vár, on the hill above Várgesztes, which has been converted into a hostel. Beds are available for passing trade as long as its dormitory has not been booked up by a group. The hostel is open all year.

Points of interest in the Vértes

Csókakői-vár
This fort was built to repel further Mongol invasions, but fell to the Ottomans in the sixteenth century. The last shots fired in anger were during the 1703–11 War of Independence, after which its strategic importance declined. Lightning destroyed one of its towers.

Mátyás-kút
This hostel was built in the 1970s for workers of the Tatabánya Cement and Lime Factory Sport Club, but is not open to passing walkers.

Mór
The settlement was founded in 1030, but by the end of the seventeenth century it had become more or less empty. In the eighteenth century Germans settled the town, and in the early nineteenth century it was almost destroyed by an earthquake.

Várgesztes
The castle on the hill above the village was the most important stronghold of the Vértes defensive line. The Ottomans captured it in 1588 and held it for almost 50 years. In the seventeenth century it was Eszterházy property, but its strategic usefulness declined. Fortunately the decay of the castle was halted in the 1930s when it was converted into a walking hostel.

Vérteskozma

Mein Gott, Mein Gott, warum hast du mich verlassen? pleads the inscription on the memorial cross at the old church. Bavarians settled here in 1744, but after World War II their descendants were repatriated to Germany. The original peasant houses are in beautiful condition, although the abandoned church and German names on the gravestones are the only reminder of the village's former residents.

Vitányvár

Like so many castles in the Vértes it was built in the thirteenth century after the Mongol invasion. During the sixteenth century the Ottomans captured it several times. Finally, in 1598 the Habsburgs blew it up to render it strategically useless.

WALK 33
Southern Vértes Escarpment

Route:	Mór – Csókakői-vár – Kopasz-hegy – Csákberény
Distance:	14km (8.5 miles)
Map:	20 Vértes 1: 40 000
Transport:	Regular buses from Csákberény back to Budapest Népliget. If taking the Csókakő diversion and hoping to catch a train back to Budapest, be aware that the railway halt is quite far from the village.
Refreshments:	Bars and buffets at Csókakő and Csákberény

This short and easy walk ascends to the southern plateau and follows the top of the escarpment. There is a diversion down through the rocky Vár-völgy to the historic castle ruin of Csókakő. The second half of the walk trails for part of the way over the open karst meadow of Pap-irtás and Kopasz-hegy, giving splendid views down to the Mór Valley.

Start at **Mór** bus station and turn right for the road to Pusztavám. The waymarks painted on the roadside telegraph poles are superfluous at this stage, but at least there is no doubt where the route is. After about 10 minutes the main road swings left, but keep straight ahead and join a rough track which eventually crosses an old railway line. Five minutes later there is a fork; take the right track through trees, leaving the last of Mór's houses behind. Continue on the red and green waymarks, but at the next fork turn right for the joint red (L) and green waymarks. From here the track rises gently through woods. Follow it round to the right, but when it begins to swing left and uphill, continue straight ahead on a path which exits the woods. At the open ground with scattered rocks there are no waymarks, but head for the other

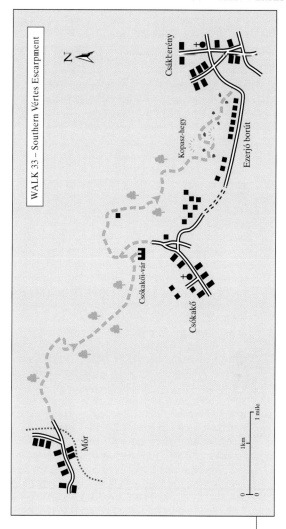

side and veer left to descend the rough steps into the
woods. Turn right to reach the bottom of a wooded

Diversion

Keep following the
Vár-völgy downhill.
Although the map
shows little of
interest, great white
outcrops and crags
rear up from the
wooded slopes
above. Visit the
castle ruin of
Csókakői-vár and
return the same way
to complete the rest
of the walk.

valley and then left to pick up the waymarks for the path traversing above the gully.

At the top the footpath becomes vague, but stay on the red (L) waymarks. The path begins to contour the escarpment and the trees give way, affording views down the Mór Valley. When the path peters out at a spur with scattered trees pick up the red (L) waymarks. From here there are two routes down to the fort of **Csókakői-vár**: a wooden sign on a tree marked *nehéz* (difficult) indicates the steep route straight down the wooded spur. Take the easier path left and down through woodland. Turn right at the main valley (Vár-völgy) to follow the good track downhill for a while. The blue waymarks mark the route from here. ◀

Retrace steps back up the valley and turn right on the green (L) waymarks which follow a track traversing around a tributary of the valley. Contouring left, the track levels at a fork. Turn right on a well-waymarked forest track. At the T-junction turn right for the main green route. At the next rather complicated junction of firebreaks and tracks find the path marked with green, green (+) and blue (triangle) waymarks. After passing the Maurer kunyhó forest cabin continue on the green (+) track and stay on this waymark.

The green (+) route turns right as a narrower path through woodland, but after a while the trees thin out and the trail crosses the meadow with scattered bushes marked Pap-irtás on the map. After passing a hill on the right with a hunting tower the track narrows and becomes a fork at the appropriately named Kopasz-hegy (Bald Mountain). Keep right, now on the green (triangle) waymarks. The footpath disappears among the bleached rocks, but the green triangles painted on the few stunted trees guide the way. After a while the waymarks lead uphill to rejoin the green (+) track. Turn right, but as the track approaches a conifer plantation and begins to swing downhill to the left, turn right for the meadow. The path descends the hill for a while, but do not descend too far; traverse left through the stand of conifers. Continue crossing a meadow and then through some more conifers. The narrow footpath contours the edge of the hill to rejoin the green (+) track. Follow the track down to the asphalt road.

Turn left for the village of Csákberény. Blue (triangle) and green (+) waymarks take the route along Kossuth út into the village centre. At the crossroads with the shop turn right for the main road, where there is a bus stop for Budapest. ▶

Extension
Instead of finishing at Csákberény, starting at the bottom of the green-(+)-waymarked track below Pap-irtás, turn right for the long Ezerjó borút, the Thousand Good Wines road, past vineyards and smallholdings back to Csókakő village.

WALK 34
Szárliget to Várgesztes

Route:	Szárliget – Vitányvár – Várgesztes
Distance:	13km (8 miles)
Map:	20 Vértes 1:40 000
Transport:	Buses from Várgesztes to the town of Tata for trains back to Budapest
Refreshments:	The bar/restaurant in the old castle at Gesztesi-vár is open to non-residents.

A section of the National Blue Route that passes through forest for the most part, although there is one good view from the castle ruin of Vitányvár. Tree carvings with a local theme guide the way, but do not make up for the bad waymarking. The route is convoluted and as a result the instructions seem complex, but keep to the waymarks where possible. Expect muddy stretches.

If starting at Szárliget railway station, cross the bridge over the platform and follow the long straight road leading diagonally into Szárliget village. After the church look for a good track peeling off down to the right. Pass the football field and cross a stream on a little bridge made from sleepers. The track rises over meadow and farmland to the main road (Highway

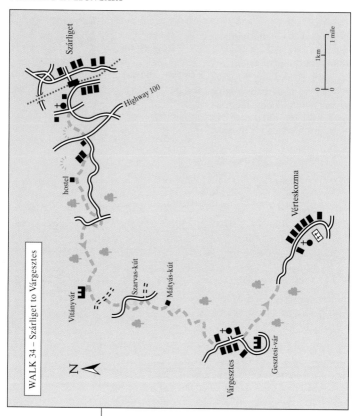

WALK 34 – Szárliget to Várgesztes

100). Cross over and head for the country road passing to the left of a restaurant. Waymarks are absent, but follow the road and turn off right for a track heading for old thatched sheep barns. The track veers left past the barns and across pasture. After the wooden cabins of a youth camp pick up the blue-waymarked path veering left into the forest. Csákányospuszta hostel is passed and the trail begins to wind uphill through the Mária-szakadék gully.

At the top of the gully the path levels and then

rises again gently to the Mária-
kép tree carving. Turn left and
follow the good track as it
rejoins the stream. After passing through a cutting the track
merges with a road coming
from the left. Follow the road
to a crossroads and take the
next turning right. After following the long straight road
for a while take the next left
on a rough track into the
woods, passing a tree carving
of a dog. From here the waymarking is poor, but after the
track swings round to the right
turn left through a cutting and
then take the first left. At the
fence and gate veer left and
uphill on a narrow path to a
broad track at the top, passing
the ruins of a rain shelter. At
the fork, turn left and down-

Vitányvár

hill. The track rises again to a crossroads. Continue
straight ahead and downhill. At the next junction
turn right. The next section descends a stony track
through a cutting with high banks. Take the first track
leaving left to traverse uphill, and at the top follow
the path along a narrow shoulder. There is a blue-
waymarked path dropping away to the left, but
ignore it for now. Look for the word *vár* or the blue
(L) waymarks painted on the trees to guide the route
to the ruined walls of **Vitányvár**.

To continue with the walk backtrack along the
ridge, but turn right to descend the blue-waymarked
path noted earlier. At the bottom turn left onto a
broader track following the green waymarks up a gentle
valley. Take the first track right for the continuation of
the Blue Route. The muddy cutting through which the
track passes can be avoided by following the left bank.

After the tree carving of Pál Rockenbauer the blue waymarks soon come to the top, where there is a forest track junction. Turn right following the good track; it soon begins to descend through a cutting. At the bottom join the asphalt road and turn left for a few paces; turn right into the woods to follow a little trail downhill along a gully. A rain shelter can be seen on the other side of the gully and the Szarvas-kút spring is passed before the trail comes out at a clearing and picnic site.

Diversion 1
For Gesztesi-vár and a welcome lunch head south along Arany J. utca and turn right where the sign for the castle indicates. Follow the asphalt road to the top of the castle hill.

There are no waymarks here, but turn sharply left to follow the overgrown track through a valley. A cave up on the slope to the right called Vörös-lyuk is passed, after which the path joins a track. Turn left and at the next crossroads of forest roads turn right. Follow the road for a few paces before picking up the blue waymarks of a trail leaving left to re-enter the forest. The trail now climbs through the woods to a junction of paths. Veer left along the undulating footpath, but as it contours to the right pick up the blue-waymarked path, dropping left to descend a very steep slope.

Diversion 2
To visit the village of Vérteskozma do not turn right for the castle but continue along Arany J. utca to the end of the village until the yellow-(square)-waymarked track takes over. Stay on the track cutting through the valley. After exiting the forest the track becomes a gravel road descending into the village.

At the bottom **Mátyás-kút** hostel is ahead. Do not go all the way down to the hostel, but take the track veering right. Turn left at the T-junction to follow a broad track on a spur. At the next fork take a right to join another track, and at the King Sigismund tree-carving bear right, picking up the blue waymarks. The rutted track winds through the forest and eventually passes a clearing. Continue until the next clearing, and turn left to cross its little meadow on a faint footpath and head for the woodland edge. Once in the forest the path joins a downhill track. It meanders around the woods for a while, but look for a well-waymarked footpath dropping to a fallen tree with another carving. Veer left and then right to pass around the tree and begin to descend a wide gully. After passing between outcrops looming up from the trees high above, the gully widens to a valley. After exiting the forest the first houses of the village are visible on the left. When the rough track joins the main road turn left for **Várgesztes**. ◀ ◀

APPENDIX 1
The Hungarian Language and Notes on Pronunciation

A Brief History

Unlike most languages in Europe, Hungarian (Magyar) is not Indo-European but belongs to the Finno-Ugrian group which has its origins east of the Ural Mountains. The details of the Magyars' early migrations are uncertain, but by the sixth century AD they had settled on the lower Don. Attacks from neighbouring tribes and a desire to be free from Kazakh rule brought the Magyars and their language to the Carpathian Basin in AD 896.

The Magyar chieftains and their christianised descendants ruled until the Ottoman invasion, but took little interest in the future survival of their language. Hungarian texts and experimental grammars were written, and the Bible was translated into Hungarian in 1590, but Latin became the language of court and officialdom. Hungarians have always shared their conquered territory with other peoples, whether the Slavic tribes they overran in the ninth century, Teutonic knights who settled in the twelfth century or nomadic Cumanians who came as refugees from the advancing Mongols in the thirteenth century. That is not to mention the import of a series of foreign kings after the Árpád dynasty died out and the annexation of much of Hungary by the Ottomans. After Habsburg forces expelled the Ottomans they introduced a settlement policy designed to exploit Hungary's natural resources and weaken the grip of the Reformation. Over 800 new German villages were built between 1711 and 1780, when the Magyar share of the total population dropped to one-third. In 1784 German became the official language and for practical purposes the day-to-day lingua franca. The settlement policy also contained a punitive aspect; many Hungarians had fought with the Ottomans, and the Habsburg administration considered the Magyars an untrustworthy bunch. The 1703–11 uprising confirmed their suspicions, and its failure resulted in exile for many Hungarian nobles and the confiscation of their estates.

With this background the survival of Hungarian as a modern workable language is a miracle. Its rescue can be attributed to the work of the Reform Movement led by the writer and poet Ferenc Kazinczy. In the late 1700s the movement transformed the Hungarian dialects into a language suitable for the modern age. In 1867, with the creation of the Dual Monarchy, Hungarian became the official language of the old kingdom. The reality on the ground offered less optimism: the linguistic map of nineteenth-century Hungary could be described as a patchwork quilt of ethnic groups who continued to converse in German, Slovakian, Serbian or Ruthenian. To counteract this situation the Hungarian administration embarked on a programme of Magyarisation at the expense of the national minorities.

Despite these efforts a little over half the population spoke Hungarian by 1900. After World War I three million Hungarians became minority citizens of states with policies hostile or indifferent to Magyar culture, an event which continues to haunt contemporary Hungarian politics. After World War II the 'collective guilt' imposed on Hungary's remaining population of German-speakers and the expulsion of thousands of families ensured that Hungarian would become the everyday language of the most secluded forest settlements, something that had not been possible before. Assimilation policies, intensive industrialisation and the centralisation of agriculture during the Communist era completed the task, creating today's more or less linguistically homogeneous state.

Hungarian's journey from Ugrian dialect to national language has been a long and remarkable one. The blood of the broad-faced nomads who crossed the Carpathians has become diluted, leaving little trace of the original Magyar. As a result Hungarians define their ethnicity in terms of an almost lost language which is now spoken by over 15 million people worldwide.

Practicalities

Hungarians make much of the Finno-Ugric connection, but after 2000 years or more of separate development Hungarian and, for example, Finnish, are mutually incomprehensible. This is hardly encouraging for the visitor to Hungary, but from a practical point of view many people in Budapest, especially the younger generation, speak English. Further, since the 1980s Russian has fallen out of favour, and Hungarian schools now focus on teaching English, and competence is also a requirement for many university degrees. Tourist offices, travel and accommodation agencies, hotels and restaurants in popular resorts have English-speaking staff. It is a different matter in the countryside, where it is a good idea to carry a phrasebook with a basic dictionary. The no-nonsense *Just Enough Hungarian* by DL Ellis and A Cheyne, published by Corvina Press, is available in English-language bookshops in Budapest. The brief introduction below will help the novice get by in most situations.

The key feature of Hungarian is its seemingly endless array of affixes bolted on to root words as well as other difficulties not worth mentioning here. To illustrate take the simple sentence: *I am going up to the mountains.* The Hungarian is *Felmegyek a hegyre. Megyek* is the first person of the verb *menni* (to go); the *Fel-* preposition transforms the verb into *I go up*; *a hegy* means *the mountain*; and the *-re* added on the end means *on to.* There is worse to come as you find that Hungarian has several suffixes for the English word *to* (*-be, -ba, -ra, -re*) when in English one will do. For example: you go *onto* Budapest (*Budapestre*) but you go *into* Eger (*Egerbe*). Sometimes it is logical. For example you go *onto* the mountains (*a hegyre*) but *into* the forest (*az erdőbe*).

There are 14 vowels and they are divided into back vowels: a, á, o, ó, u, ú; and front vowels: e, é, i, í, ö, ő, ü, ű. There is a tendency for groups of vowels in words and their suffixes to harmonise according to these two groups. So the root *erdő* (forest) is dominated by front vowels (e, ő) therefore the suffix harmonises: *erdőbe*. This is a general rule, but there are plenty of exceptions when it comes to place-names. *Budapest*, for example, is dominated by back vowels (a, u) but the suffix agrees with the final vowel (e), thus *Budapestre*. The good news is that bus drivers and ticket sellers will know what you mean even if you get the suffix wrong.

There is little time on a short walking holiday to master anything more basic than greetings and numbers. Pronunciation is the most important thing to get right, especially when buying travel tickets. Carry a notebook. If you are not confident that you will ever pronounce tongue twisters like Sátoraljaújhely, write it down for the bus driver or merely point to the map. The following aid to pronunciation and the list of useful words and phrases are designed to guide the walker around Hungary with little fuss or information overload.

Aid to Pronunciation

Hungarian words may appear difficult to pronounce at first, but unlike English the system is logical and there are few exceptions to the rule. Just take your time and remember that accents lengthen vowels and consonants are harder and shorter than in English. Double consonants (tt, gg, dd, etc.) tend to make the sound longer and harder.

Vowels

a As in 'car'.

á As in 'spa' but a little longer.

e Short like 'met'.

é Lengthened to become the 'a' in 'say'.

i The short double 'e' in 'feet'.

í The long double 'e' in 'see'.

o The 'o' sound in 'ought'.

ó As in 'foe'.

ö The short 'e' in 'her'.

ő Lengthen the 'ö'.

u The short double 'o' in 'foot'.

ú The long double 'o' in 'food'.

ü Similar to the German 'über'.

ű Lengthened 'ü'.

Consonants

b As in English but harder.

c A short and sharp sound, like the 'ts' ending of 'bats'.

cs Like the 'ch' sound in 'church'.

d A harder English 'd'.

f Short as in 'fat'.

g Hard as in 'get'.

gy Soft like the 'd' in 'dew'.

h Never drop it – always like 'hat'.

j As in German, pronounced as 'y'.

k Hard, like the 'c' in 'cat'.

l As in 'let'.

ly The 'y' in 'hay'.

m As in English.

n As in English.

ny The 'n' sound in 'nuisance' or 'cognac'.

p As in English, but harder.

r Rolled like the Scots 'r'.

s Always the 'sh' in 'ship'.

sz As the English 's' in 'sit'.

t As in English but harder.

ty Somewhere between 'chew' and 'tube'.

v Shorter than English 'v'.

w Only in borrowed words – the same as 'v'.

x Only in borrowed words – same as English.

y When at the end of names, it replaces 'i'.

z As in 'zebra'.

zs A soft sound, like the 'g' in 'beige'.

APPENDIX 2
Glossary of Useful Words and Phrases

Emergencies

Help!	Segítség!
Fire!	Tűz!

Keep it simple

Do you speak English?	Beszél mayarul?
I would like this one.	Ezt kérem.
I would like that one.	Azt kérem.
I want to go here.	Ide akarok menni.
How much is it?	Mennyibe kerül?
Write it down for me, please.	Írja le, kérem!

Basics and greetings

Yes	Igen
No	Nem
Good morning!	Jó reggelt!
Good day!	Jó napot!
Good evening!	Jó estét!
Good night!	Jó éjszakát!
Good-bye! (Formal)	Viszontlátásra!
Good-bye! (Slightly informal)	Viszlát!
Hello!/Bye! (Very informal)	Szia!
Kiss your hands! (Child's greeting to adult or adult to older woman)	Csókolom!
Thank you.	Köszönöm.
Excuse me! (Attracting attention or squeezing past)	Elnézést!
I'm sorry. (If you bump into someone or stand on their toes)	Bocsánat
I'm terribly sorry (Appropriate humility for ticket inspectors)	Nagyon sajnálom

Numbers

zero	nulla
one	egy
two	kettő
three	három
four	négy
five	öt
six	hat
seven	hét
eight	nyolc
nine	kilenc
ten	tíz
eleven	tizenegy
twelve, thirteen, etc.	tizenkettő, tizenhárom, etc.
twenty	húsz
twenty-one, twenty-two, etc.	huszonegy, huszonkettő, etc.
thirty	harminc
thirty-one, forty-one, etc.	harmincegy, negyvenegy, etc.
forty	negyven
fifty	ötven
sixty	hatvan
seventy	hetven
eighty	nyolcvan
ninety	kilencven
hundred	száz
thousand	ezer

Days of the week

Monday	hétfő
Tuesday	kedd
Wednesday	szerda
Thursday	csütörtök
Friday	péntek
Saturday	szombat
Sunday	vasárnap

Travel signs

(nem) dohányzó	*(non) smoking*
Érkező/Érkezés/Érkeznek	*arrivals*
Hova/Hová	*destination*
Induló/Indulás/Indulnak	*departures*
menetrend	*timetable*
Mikor	*departure time*

pénztár	*ticket office*
repülőtér	*airport*
vágány	*platform*

Travel questions

Can I have a ticket to Pécs?	Kérek egy jegyet Pécsre!
Where is the (Pécs) train?	Hol van a (pécsi) vonat?
Where does this train/bus go?	Hová megy ez a vonat/busz?
When does it leave?	Mikor indul?
Does this bus/train stop at Pécs?	Megáll ez a busz/vonat Pécsen?
(Is this seat) free?	Szabad?

Timetable footnotes

hétköznapokon	*runs on week days*
munkanapokon	*runs on working days*
szabadnapokon	*runs on weekends and holidays*
szabadnapok kivételével naponta	*runs every day except weekends and holidays*
szombaton	*runs on Saturdays*
vasárnap	*runs on Sundays*

Intercity tickets

kocsi	*carriage number*
hely	*seat number*

Accommodation

Is there a room for	Van szoba…?
…tonight?	…ma éjszakára?
…two nights?	…két éjszakára?
…one week?	…egy hétre?
I leave tomorrow	Holnap már megyek
single/double room	egyágyas/kétágyas szoba
Is there a place to put my tent?	Van sátorhely?
How much is it?	Mennyibe kerül?
Are/Is there…?	Van…?
…bedding?	…ágynemű?
…a towel?	…törölköző?
…heating?	…fűtés?
There is none	nincs/nincsen
cold	hideg
hot	meleg

Miscellaneous

Could you help me?	Segítene kérem?
I am lost	Eltévedtem
Where is the…?	Hol van a …?
phone	telefon
phone card	telefonkártya
toilet	mosdó/WC

Places to eat or drink

büfé/falatozó	*stand up/take away snack bar*
csárda	*country restaurant*
étterem, vendéglő	*restaurant*
kávézó, kávéház/cukrászda	*café/ pastry shop*
borozó	*wine bar*
söröző, kocsma, presszó, italbolt	*pub*

Places to buy food

bolt, vegyes bolt,	*shop*
zöldség(es), zöldség-gyümölcs	*greengrocer*

In the restaurant

The menu, please	Kérem az étlapot!
Excuse me! (for the waiter)	Elnézést!
Can I have the bill, please?	A számlát kérném!

In the village bar

I would like…	Kérek…
…a bottle of beer	…egy üveg sört
…a large glass of beer	…egy korsó sört
…a small glass of beer	…egy pohár sört
…a coffee	…egy kávét
…an orange juice	…egy narancslét
…a mineral water	…egy ásványvizet
…a large glass of red wine	…egy nagy pohár vörös bort
…a small glass of white wine	…egy kis pohár fehér bort
…a wine and soda	…egy fröccsöt

Drinks	**Italok**
beer	sör
bottled	üveges
draught	csapolt
lager	világos
stout	barna

fruit brandy	pálinka
fruit juice	gyümölcslé
soda water	szóda
soft drinks	üdítő
tap water	csapvíz
wine	bor
demi-sec	félédes
dry	száraz
red	vörös
sweet	édes
white	fehér

Breakfast at a family house

bacon	szalonna
bap/roll	zsemle
bread	kenyér
breakfast	reggeli
butter	vaj
coffee	kávé
eggs	tojás
...boiled	főtt
...fried	tükörtojás
...scrambled	rántotta

frankfurters	virsli
ham and eggs	sonka tojással *or* 'ham and eggs'
honey	méz
jam	lekvár
milk	tej
sausage	kolbász
tea	tea *(pronounce the 'a')*
toast	pirítós

Noticeboards

Belépés csak engedéllyel!	*Enter Only With Permission!*
Belépni tilos!	*No Entry!*
Életveszélyes!	*Life Threatening!*
(Nem) Ivóvíz	*(Not) Drinking Water*
Magánterület	*Private Property*
Nem működik/Rossz	*Out of Order*
Nyitva	*Open*
Zárva	*Closed*
Vigyázz! Villanypásztor!	*Beware! Electric fence*
Tüzet rakni tilos!	*No Fires!*

APPENDIX 3
Glossary of Hungarian Topographical Terms

Words in Map Keys

Autóbuszvonal megállóval	*bus stop*
Barlang	*cave*
Benzintöltő-állomás	*petrol station, garage*
Eligazító tábla	*direction sign*
Elsősegélyhely	*first aid centre*
Emlékmű	*monument, statue*
Erdőgazdasági üzemi út	*forestry service road*
Eséstüske	*outcrop from spur*
Esőház	*rain shelter*
Facsoport; liget	*group of trees; glade*
Fasor; bokorsor	*tree-lined street; bushes*
Földút	*unmetalled road, track*
Földvár	*earth fort*
Gát	*dyke*
Gémeskút	*crane well*
Gépkocsiszervíz	*garage*
Halomsírmező	*grave mounds*
Horhos	*gully*
Javított földút	*improved unmetalled road*
Jelentősebb rom	*significant ruin*
Jellegzetes szikla	*characteristic crag, cliff*
Jól tájékoztató magányos fa	*solitary tree, landmark*
Kápolna	*chapel*
Kastély	*mansion, manor house*
Kemping	*campsite (organised)*
Kereszt/Képoszlop	*wayside cross/ carved post*
Kilátó	*look-out point, tower*

Kórház	*hospital*
Kő-, karrmező	*boulder field, karst meadow*
Kút	*well, fountain, pump*
Magasles	*hunting tower, hide*
Metsződés	*gully*
Nemzeti Park határa	*National Park boundary*
Ösvény	*path, trail, lane*
Pihenőhely	*rest-, picnic site*
Romos épület	*ruins*
Sánc	*rampart, mound, earthwork*
Sípálya	*ski-run*
Sír	*grave*
Síút	*ski route*
Szálloda	*hotel*
Szekérút	*cart road, track*
Sziklafal	*rocks, cliff*
Szobor	*statue*
Táborozó-/Sátorozóhely	*camping spot*
Templom	*church*
Tereplépcső	*terracing*
Toronyszerű építmény	*tower, TV/ radio mast*
Töltés	*dyke*
Turistaház	*hostel*
Vadetető	*wild game feeder*
Vár/várrom	*fort, castle/ruin*
Védett	*protected*
Zsomboly	*sink-hole*

Common Topographical Terms

alja	*bottom of (hill/mountain)*
alsó	*lower*
árok	*gully, trench*
bánya	*mine, quarry*
bérc	*ridge*
bükk	*beech*
csemetekert	*tree nursery*
csúcs	*peak, top*
domb	*hill*
dűlő	*hillock*
erdészház	*forest house*
erdészlak	*forest cabin*
erdő	*forest, wood*

fa	*tree*
felső	*upper*
fogadó	*inn*
folyó	*river*
forrás	*spring*
föld(ek)	*ground(s), land(s)*
halomsír	*grave mound*
hegy	*mountain*
hideg	*cold*
ifjúsági tábor	*youth camp*
irtás	*clearing*
kapu	*gate*
kaszáló	*grazing meadow*
kert	*garden*
kilátóhely	*look-out point*
kő/kövek	*stone/rocks*
kőbánya	*stone quarry*
kőfülke	*rock crevice, cave*
kulcsosház	*cabin or cottage for hire*
kunyhó	*cabin*
láp	*marsh, bog*
lyuk	*hole, sink-hole, cave*
malom	*mill*
medence	*basin*
mező	*meadow, clearing*
nyereg	*saddle, col*
nyiladék	*glade, firebreak*
oldal	*side*
őrház	*guardhouse*
panzió	*small hotel*
parkerdő	*forest park*
patak	*stream*
pihenő	*resting place/picnic site*
pincesor	*row of wine cellars*
puszta	*plain, bleak, bare*
régi vasút	*old railway (course of)*
rét	*meadow*
rom	*ruin*
Római út	*Roman road*
síugró	*ski-jump*
síút	*ski-run*
szép kilátás!	*Beautiful view!*
szikla	*rock*
szőlő	*vineyard*

szurdok	*gorge, ravine*
tanösvény	*study path*
tanya	*small farm*
tábor	*camp*
tájház	*village museum*
telep	*works, plant*
tető	*peak, top*
tisztás	*clearing*
tó	*lake*
töbör	*sink-hole*
tölgy	*oak*
üdülő	*former trade union hostel*
út	*road, way*
utca	*street*
vadászház	*hunters' cabin*
vadászkastély	*hunting lodge*
vágás	*cutting, felled area*
vár	*castle, fort*
várrom	*castle-, fort ruin*
vendégház	*guesthouse*
víznyelő	*gully*
volt	*former, formerly known as*
völgy	*valley*
zug	*hollow*

Common Abbreviations Used on Maps

bg.	*cave*
csr.	*restaurant*
eh.	*forest house*
el.	*forest cabin*
eml.	*monument*
f.	*spring*
h.	*mountain, hill*
kny.	*cabin*
mjr.	*manor farm*
p.	*stream*
pu.	*main rail or bus station*
th.	*walkers' hostel*
Tsz.	*agricultural co-operative*
TVK	*Landscape Protection Area*
TVT	*Nature Conservation Area*
Üd.	*trade union hostel*
Vá.	*railway station*
Vh.	*hunters' lodge*
VI.	*hunters' cabin*
v.m.	*railway halt*

APPENDIX 4
Useful Addresses and Telephone Numbers

EMERGENCY SERVICES

General helpline (multi-lingual) 112

ACCOMMODATION

Falusi és Agroturizmus Országos Szövetsége (Hungarian Federation of Rural and Agricultural Tourism)

Budapest (District 7)
Király utca 93
Tel: + 36 1 352 1433
Fax: + 36 1 352 9804

Centre of
Hungarian Tourism
www.falutur.hu

TOURINFORM

24-hour hotline (from abroad): +36 60 55 00 44

24-hour line (within Hungary): 06 80 66 00 44 (toll free)

www.tourinform.hu

www.hungarytourism.hu

Budapest (District 5)
Vörösmarty tér
(open 24 hours)

Budapest (District 5)
Sütő utca 2
Tel: 1 317 9800
Fax: 1 317 9656

Budapest (District 6)
Liszt Ferenc tér 11
Tel: 1 322 4098
Fax: 1 342 9390

Budapest (District 7)
Király utca 93
Tel: 1 352 1433
Fax: 1 352 9804

Budapest (District 6)
Nyugati pályaudvar
(Western Railway
Station)
Tel: 1 302 8580
Fax: 1 302 8580

Bakony
Veszpém 8200
Vár utca 4
Tel: 88 401 229
Fax: 88 404 548

Zirc 8420
Rákóczi tér 1
Tel: 88 416 816
Fax: 88 416 817

Balaton
Badacsonytomaj 8261
Park utca 6
Tel: 87 431 046
Fax: 87 431 046

Balatonfüred 8230
Szécheny utca 47
Tel: 87 482 577
Fax: 87 580 481

Révfülöp 8253
Villa Filip tér 8/b
Tel: 87 463 092
Fax: 87 463 092

Tapolca 8300
Deák Ferenc utca 20
Tel: 87 510 777
Fax: 87 510 778

Bükk
Eger 3300
Dobó tér 2
Tel: 36 517 715
Fax: 36 518 815

Miskolc 3500
Mindszent tér 1
Tel: 46 348 921
Fax: 46 348 921

Mezőkövesd 3400
Szent László tér 23
Tel: 49 500 285
Fax: 49 500 286

Mátra
Gyöngyös 3200
Fő tér 10
Tel: 37 311 155
Fax: 37 311 155

Mecsek
Pécs 7621
Széchenyi tér 9
Tel: 72 213 315
Fax: 72 212 632

Kárász 7333
Petőfi utca 36
Tel: 72 420 074
Fax: 72 420 074

Pilis
Szentendre 2000
Dumtsa Jenő utca 22
Tel: 26 317 965
Fax: 26 317 965

Zemplén
Sátoraljaújhely 3980
Táncsics tér 3
Tel: 47 321 458
Fax: 47 321 458

EMBASSIES

UK
Budapest (District 5)
Harmincad utca 6
Tel: 1 266 2888
www.britishembassy.hu

USA
Budapest (District 5)
Szabadság tér 12
Tel: 1 475 4400
www.usis.hu

Australia
Budapest (District 12)
Királyhágó tér 8/9
Tel: 1 201 9792
www.ausembbp.hu

New Zealand
Budapest (District 6)
Teréz körút 38
Tel: 1 331 4908

South Africa
Budapest (District 2)
Gárdonyi Géza utca 17
Tel: 1 392 0999

PUBLIC TRANSPORT

MÁV
(Central booking office)
Budapest (District 6)
Andrássy út 35
www.elvira.hu

VOLÁN (Hungarian
State Bus Company)
www.volan.hu

MAPS

Cartographia
Budapest (District 6)
Bajcsy-Zsilinszky út 37

WALKING CLUBS

MTSZ
Budapest (District 6)
Bajcsy-Zsilinszky út 31

WALKING SHOPS

Mountex
Budapest (District 7)
Üllői út 7

Mountex
Budapest (District 2)
Margit körút 61-63

Tengerszem
Budapest (District 6)
Teréz körút 33

Tengerszem
Budapest (District 7)
Dohány utca 29

Mountex
Miskolc 3525
Széchenyi út 21

LISTING OF CICERONE GUIDES

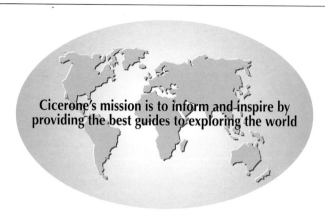

Cicerone's mission is to inform and inspire by providing the best guides to exploring the world

Since its foundation over 30 years ago, Cicerone has specialised in publishing guidebooks and has built a reputation for quality and reliability. It now publishes nearly 300 guides to the major destinations for outdoor enthusiasts, including Europe, UK and the rest of the world.

Written by leading and committed specialists, Cicerone guides are recognised as the most authoritative. They are full of information, maps and illustrations so that the user can plan and complete a successful and safe trip or expedition – be it a long face climb, a walk over Lakeland fells, an alpine traverse, a Himalayan trek or a ramble in the countryside.

With a thorough introduction to assist planning, clear diagrams, maps and colour photographs to illustrate the terrain and route, and accurate and detailed text, Cicerone guides are designed for ease of use and access to the information.

If the facts on the ground change, or there is any aspect of a guide that you think we can improve, we are always delighted to hear from you.

Cicerone Press
2 Police Square Milnthorpe Cumbria LA7 7PY
Tel:01539 562 069   Fax:01539 563 417
e-mail:info@cicerone.co.uk   web:www.cicerone.co.uk

CICERONE